DOGMAN DECLASSIFIED

THE UNFINISHED STORY OF THE DOGMAN

W.J. BRENDLE, PH.D.

Published by Beyond The Fray Publishing

ISBN 13: 979-8-89234-151-6

Full cover created by L. Douglas Hogan

Printed in the USA

Beyond The Fray Publishing, a division of Beyond The Fray, LLC, San Diego, CA
www.beyondthefraypublishing.com

SINCE 2018

CONTENTS

PREFACE

The unknown has always beckoned to humanity, calling to us from the depths of shadowed forests and the murky edges of our reality. For centuries, people have told stories of creatures that defy classification. The beasts which move through the night glimpsed only in fleeting moments of terror. Such myths have fascinated, inspired, and baffled those who have heard their tale. These tales have inspired an enduring desire to hear more of the secrets that lie just over the rim of our knowledge. One such myth is the myth of the Dogman, the beast that has entered the fabric of modern-day folklore, its reality a testament to the tenacity of the human mind.

This book results from my own curiosity and persistent search for the truth. When I first heard of the Dogman, I wrote it off as another exaggerated legend, a result of folklore that had been embellished and distorted over the years. But the more I looked into the topic, the more I found a broad and unexpectedly uniform corpus of eyewitness testimony dating back decades. These testimonies were not just from anybody, but from hunters, police officers, and individuals who had no motive to fabricate such experiences. What did they witness? An elaborate hoax, mistaken identity, or something beyond the realm of conventional explanation? And so, as I began to compile and understand the facts, I realized the Dogman was not just a legend. It is also a multiform and multifaceted phenomenon which has intrigued so many.

I am not the type of individual who will say that they have all the answers. This book is an investigative expedition into the mysteries of an ancient conundrum. I do not intend to persuade you to accept the Dogman, but to lie out the evidence as it currently exists. It is for you to review and allow you to develop your own views. By historical research, scientific analysis, and eyewitness account, we shall try to divide fact from fancy, to discover the truth of a legend that has long been in suspense. Some will dismiss cryptozoology as the product of fantasy. But history has taught us that some monsters once consigned myths, such as the giant squid or the mountain gorilla, were eventually discovered and proven to exist. Can the same be said of the Dogman? What motivates individuals to report on seeing such a beast, and why does the legend persist?

As you turn these pages, I encourage you to approach this subject with a healthy skepticism and an open mind. You are perhaps a card-carrying believer, a questioning skeptic, or a person reading this story of the Dogman for the very first time. Whatever the case, I encourage you to join me. The reality might be impossible to attain, but it is the quest for the truth which makes the unknown so compelling. As we travel into the realm of the Dogman, we will be forced to refer to a wide range of opinions and interpretations, from the scientific to the paranormal. We will examine the alternative explanations and theories that have been proposed to explain the Dogman and evaluate the evidence for or against each. When we finally arrive at the destination of our journey, we will have gained more insight into the Dogman and how it features in modern folklore. And we will have revealed the many secrets about this elusive animal.

Welcome to this Dogman quest, and let's embark on this journey together. Along the way, we'll encounter a seemingly simple yet profound question: what lies beyond the boundaries of our knowledge, on the fringes of existence? I believe the answer is a mystery waiting to be unraveled, a mystery that has captivated human beings for centuries and continues to ignite our imagination and curiosity. Join me on this expedition into the unknown, and together, let's uncover the truth behind the Dogman legend.

- W.J. Brendle, Ph.D.

CHAPTER 1
HISTORICAL ACCOUNTS OF DOGMAN

The Dogman is a cryptid in contemporary folklore. But its past seems to run deeper than we realize. There are centuries-old legends of dog-headed creatures and dog type hybrids. They were found in most ancient cultures throughout the globe. Egypt, for instance, had Anubis, the god with a jackal head. Greek literature and mythology included such animals, too. Things such as the Cynocephali who were men in body and dog in head. As time went by, this depicts a common theme of human-like dog-like beings.

The Mesopotamians had the 'Lamassu,' a dog-headed person with the body of a lion. The Mesopotamians worshipped this divine animal as a protector and guardian. Norse mythology possesses the 'Fenrir,' an enormous wolf-like creature who was dreaded for his strength because only evil would arise from it. These myths speak of a very ancient tryst between humanoid and hybrid creatures and how they may have influenced the imagination of men.

There are thousands of reports and sightings of what we currently refer to as of the Dogman. It is seen as a man-like animal with dog-like features, but if it exists at all is questionable. Its cultural influence, however, is not. Most of the globe had never even heard of it until the latter part of the 20th century. Some believe it has existed along Michigan's Manistee River since the days of the Odawa tribes. No matter if it's true or not, the legend keeps increasing.

ANCIENT EGYPT

Anubis is the jackal-headed, mysterious one who is ever watchful over the dead. There are few figures in ancient Egyptian mythology who evoke the same mixture of awe and apprehension. He is the guardian of the dead, who then silently escorts souls into the afterlife. Half-man, half-beast, his form blurred the line between human intelligence and animal instinct, a living bridge between the tangible and the unknown. His image, a muscular human frame crowned with the sleek, pointed ears of a jackal, was more than mere artistry. It was a warning, a promise, a symbol of the Egyptians' relentless attempt to decipher the riddles of life and death.

Why a jackal one may wonder. The answer lies in the creature's relentless presence on the fringes of civilization, scavenging the remains of the departed, haunting the barren wastes beyond the reach of human settlement. The ancients saw in this nocturnal predator not just death but a duty. A keeper of thresholds, a guardian of the liminal space between existence and oblivion. Yet, some scholars suggest something deeper, something primal. Perhaps Anubis was more than a simple personification of the feared desert scavenger. Maybe he emerged from a universal human archetype. A long buried, now forgotten memory of a shadowy guardian standing at the crossroads of life and death.

And then there's a more unsettling possibility. What if Anubis wasn't entirely a myth? Legends of hybrid beings, part human and part beast, are not unique to Egypt. They appear across cultures, spanning millennia. Could the Egyptians have glimpsed something, or at least heard whispers of a creature that blurred the line between man and jackal? A precursor to the Dogman legends, a spectral figure stalking the sands long before its echoes reached other mythologies. The answer to this we may never know. But in a world where myth and reality intertwine, where the boundaries of imagination and experience remain tantalizingly unclear, the question lingers.

Historians tell us Egyptian mythology is full of hybrid beings. Their human-animal forms are a mixture of cosmic forces and divine mysteries. Anubis is no exception as he thrived in a pantheon where the blending of animals and humans was normal. Where gods had the heads of falcons, crocodiles, and jackals with each of these features steeped in symbolism. This anthropomorphic combination wasn't just artistic freedom, it reflected how ancient peoples interpreted the existence of gods. A world where the known and unknown, the rational and the irrational, were deeply mixed. Even now those combinations still compel us, with mysteries we've yet to unravel.

Anubis's importance stretches far beyond his role as a guardian of the dead and a deity. He is the doorway and the guide between the razor-thin veil of the living and the dead. As the god of mummification, he secures the dead's passage into the afterlife. His presence was an assurance that the soul's journey would not end in oblivion. To the living, he was an arbiter of justice, weighing hearts against the feather of Ma'at, a task that demanded both mercy and cold impartiality. Protector or executioner, well, he was both, and there lay his powers.

There are many conflicts in what define him. He soothes you but yet he terrifies you, a beacon of light in the void of darkness and yet he is the inescapable finality. His appearance has those piercing canine eyes and the sleek obsidian like fur. His presence alone commands reverence, awe, and perhaps even some primal fear. And yet, historians across time have fixated on him, drawn to his conflicting nature. Is it his control over death that holds us, or the eerie familiarity of his duality? Perhaps it is his pushing and pulling between fear and comfort, of loss but yet a hope of an afterlife.

Hybrid and humanoid figures dominate Egyptian art, and their presence suggests more than mere artistic freedom. There are beings with falcon heads, lion torsos, or crocodile limbs to signify forces beyond the human grasp. These creatures are bridges between the mundane and the supernatural. The selection of canine traits for Anubis was not random; people revered dogs for their vigilance and unwavering loyalty. The jackal thrived in the liminal spaces and the Egyptians feared and revered the desert's edge. But could these depictions hint at something more?

Some of the ancient Egyptian artifacts raise tantalizing questions. There are many sculptures of bipedal canine figures etched in stone with unsettling precision. Are they a mere allegory, or did they originate from firsthand sightings now lost to time? Did the ancients stone masons carve what they imagined or what they encountered? The answer is like Anubis himself, remaining elusive, locked within a past that refuses to fully surrender its secrets.

ANCIENT GREECE

The Cynocephali are one of the most mysterious and enduring creatures in ancient Greek and Roman mythology being described as dog-headed people. They appear in many writings of the ancient Greek historians. Ancient accounts depict them as humanoid creatures with canine heads who lived in distant lands beyond the known world. Many scholars, mythologists, and cryptozoologist have found the Cynocephali fascinating, whether viewed as savage warriors, noble protectors, or just cautionary symbols of the unknown.

This race of dog headed people are a mysterious and enigmatic group of cryptid beings. The works of ancient Greek historians contain the first recorded accounts of these dog-headed men. Men who created the maps to document the peoples and creatures of the world included them. In his seminal work, *Histories* (5th century BCE), Herodotus, often called the "Father of History," provided captivating descriptions of these fantastical beings, enabling later writers to elaborate on them.

Ctesias was a Greek physician and historian who served at the Persian court in the 5th century BCE. His now-lost work, *Indica*, contains one of the most vivid descriptions of the Cynocephali. He based his information on the reports taken from travelers and traders. He was sure the Cynocephali roamed the lower parts of India, tucked away in remote forests and jagged hills. People said they lived off the land, fast and fierce, chasing prey, foraging, surviving without help from the outside world. But there was another side to them, one that didn't fit the image of wild isolation. They were trading with other civilizations. Somehow, despite their seclusion, they bartered with others, using gestures and signs instead of words.

Ctesias described the Cynocephali as fierce warriors, strong and deadly in battle. They carried powerful weapons, moved with precision, and fought with skill sharpened by generations in the wild. It was said that no one faced them without fear. But it seems they were more than just fighters. Travelers swore they understood the land better than anyone, reading the earth, the wind, the signs of nature like a language of their own. Other civilizations viewed their land as harsh and unlivable. But yet it was simply home to them. Greek historians documented and wrote of these fascinating people living in a land where others would fail.

Legends claimed that the Cynocephali's unique physical characteristics of dog-like heads and human bodies resulted from their believed closeness to the ancient gods. According to the various legends, the Cynocephali were the offspring of the god Apollo. It is said Apollo had given them the powers of speed, strength, and agility. People believed their physical appearance illustrated their divine heritage. This set them apart from other human societies and made them a subject of both fascination and fear.

Ctesias and other ancient historians wrote detailed accounts of the Cynocephali, yet they remain nothing more than a mystery being caught somewhere between myth and reality. Did they exist at all? Some say they were inspired by real tribes, their features exaggerated over time. Others dismiss them as pure legend, a story meant to entertain or warn.

Still, the Cynocephali were everywhere in Greek art and stories. Artists captured them in ways that stirred admiration, awe, and fear. Some tales painted them as being fast and ruthless, warriors impossible to defeat. Others cast them as noble protectors, guarding sacred places or serving as mercenaries for kings.

But not all the stories were kind. Many described them as wild, uncivilized, more beast than man. Was this how the Greeks saw the so-called "barbarians" beyond their borders? However, in this context, the dog-headed people would simply symbolize the dangers of the unknown. The perceived moral and cultural inferiority of foreign peoples. This depiction of them being barking and animalistic beings reinforced the idea of their "strangeness". Did this possibly serve as a cautionary tale about venturing too far from your own land and the known world?

Our modern-day descriptions of the Dogman seem to draw some striking parallels to the Cynocephali. Both legends emphasize the creatures' humanoid stature with canine features, and a marginal existence between humanity and the wild. Descriptions often portray both beings as fiercely territorial and capable of great violence. Yet they are also sometimes portrayed as protective or even noble. Could these parallels suggest the Cynocephali may be an ancient archetype, rooted in humanity's newer fascination with canine traits?

The Cynocephali legend has long been a fascination of scholars and cryptid enthusiasts alike. One of the most intriguing theories surrounding this mysterious being is that genuine sightings of an unknown or extinct species have inspired it. It is easy for us to imagine that ancient civilizations may have encountered a primate or hominid species that possessed canine-like features. Thus, sparking the creation of myths and legends such as that of the Cynocephali.

There is currently no fossil evidence to support this hypothesis. It remains a compelling plausibility for those who view mythology as a record of ancient encounters with the unexplained. An idea where myths and legends may be based on actual events or encounters with unknown species is compelling. Many scholars and researchers have explored this. By examining the cultural and historical contexts in which these myths grew, we may be able to uncover clues about the origins of the Cynocephali and other similar creatures.

One of the most intriguing aspects of this theory is the possibility that the Cynocephali may have been inspired by a now-extinct primate species. Researchers believe this species lived in ancient India and Southeast Asia. Researchers have unearthed many species of ancient primates and hominids in this area, resulting in a rich and diverse fossil record. Is it possible that one of these species may have possessed canine-like features? Possibly one with a protruding jaw or teeth that were exaggerated or distorted in the retelling of myths and legends?

The heart of the Cynocephali myth lies the concept of liminality. For a long time, people have considered dogs and wolves creatures of the spaces between worlds: domesticated yet wild, loyal yet dangerous. This duality makes them a powerful symbol in human culture, representing the boundaries between life and death, civilization and wilderness, and the known and the unknown.

The Cynocephali, the dog-headed people, took this symbolism one step further. By combining human and canine traits, they became literal embodiments of liminality. They were not fully human, yet not entirely animal. Their role as being both noble and savages underscores this ambiguity. On the one hand, people admired them for their strength, courage, and loyalty; on the other, they were in fear of their ferocity and strangeness.

THE ROMAN EMPIRE AND EARLY CHRISTIAN ACCOUNTS

The Romans, with their vast empire and insatiable curiosity, inherited much from Greek culture, including the tales of the Cynocephali. Roman explorers and mapmakers, eager to expand their knowledge of the world, often embellished accounts of these dog-headed men, placing them in uncharted territories as symbols of the unknown. This was not surprising, given the Romans' natural inclination for mythmaking and their desire to create a sense of wonder and awe around the world they sought to conquer. By depicting the Cynocephali as mysterious and exotic creatures, the Romans were able to create a sense of distance and otherness, reinforcing their own cultural superiority. This fed the idea of the Roman Empire as a beacon of civilization.

Unlike the Greeks, who portrayed the Cynocephali as formidable warriors, Roman accounts often depicted them as lessor warriors and exotic creatures. The Romans saw the Cynocephali as a manifestation of the unknown, a reminder of the dangers and uncertainties that lay beyond the boundaries of their empire. By portraying them as strange and exotic creatures, the Romans were able to reinforce their own sense of identity and purpose. While also creating a sense of fascination and wonder around the world, they sought to conquer. The Romans were said to have created an uneasy truce with them centuries before the Second Macedonian War in 197 BCE.

Early Christianity added new layers to these myths, incorporating the Cynocephali into the Christian narrative as a symbol of the transformative power of faith. Saint Christopher, one of the most fascinating figures in Christian tradition, was in early orthodoxy, depicted with the head of a dog in ancient texts and iconography. According to legend, he was a Cynocephalus before his conversion, symbolizing the transformative power of faith to civilize even the most "beastly" of beings.

The persistence of Cynocephali myths into the Middle Ages, fueled by explorers' accounts and the continued fascination with the unknown, ensured their place in the collective imagination for centuries. As European explorers and missionaries ventured into the unknown, they brought back tales of strange and exotic creatures, which were incorporated into the existing mythology of the Cynocephali. This created a sense of continuity and connection between the ancient world and the modern era. Keeping the myths and legends of the past alive continued to shape the imagination of people in the present.

The Christian interpretation of the Cynocephali also reflected the broader cultural and theological concerns of the time. The idea of the transformative power of faith, as embodied by Saint Christopher, was a powerful symbol of the Christian message. A message that emphasized the idea that even the most "beastly" of beings could be redeemed through the power of faith. This narrative also reinforced the idea of the Christian as a civilized and enlightened beings. People who were capable of transcending the limitations of the natural world through the power of faith.

In the Middle Ages, the Cynocephali continued to be a popular subject in art and literature, appearing in illuminated manuscripts, tapestries, and other forms of visual art. They were often depicted as strange and exotic creatures, with dog-like heads and bodies, but also with human-like features and abilities. This ambivalence towards the Cynocephali reflects the complex and multifaceted nature of medieval culture, which was characterized by a deep sense of wonder and awe for the natural world. But also, a profound fear of the unknown and the unexplained.

OTHER CIVILIZATIONS AND PARALLELS

The Mesopotamian Sumerians, who were among the first civilizations to make an impression, wrote about hybrid animals in the *Epic of Gilgamesh,* one of the greatest books of ancient literature. Not necessarily a dog, but with the same themes: combining human and animal characteristics to represent divine strength or forces of nature. The Sumerians, between circa 4500-1900 BCE, were the highly religious individuals spiritually with a wonderful sense of nature and the powers which governed it.

The Sumerians documented a variety of monsters in the *Epic of Gilgamesh,* which were hybrids, and each had particular qualities and symbolic values. Several creatures were endowed with the strength and ferocity of lions and some with wolves' cunning and craftiness. They were emissaries or messengers of the gods and wielded the strength and authority of the gods that man could not even begin to comprehend.

Sumerian hybrid mythology was not specific to the *Epic of Gilgamesh,* however, but was repeated and reiterated in all of their mythology and art. Their gods, as part of Sumerian mythology, also manifested themselves as hybrid in form, blending human with animal characteristics and creating figures that were powerful and imposing. One example is the god Enlil. He was believed to be the master of the winds and the air. He was sometimes described as a lion-man hybrid to represent his authority and control over nature.

In Vedic India, there are ancient texts which expose a rich list of mythological monsters. Monsters like the Krittikas, animals who are deeply linked with the wolves and their ferocity. These enigmatic creatures, although not really similar to the Cynocephali or European werewolf folklore, might have had some discreet impact about tales of men possessing dog heads.

The Vedic age ranges from around 1500 to 500 BCE. This was a time of highly developed cultural and philosophical bloom in India. The time when sacred texts like the *Rigveda* and the *Mahabharata* were composed. These texts include some of the oldest known Indian myths and legends and are excellent sources of information on the religion and culture of the Vedic civilization.

The Krittikas, in these Vedic scriptures presented here, have been portrayed as mysterious and fierce beings, parallel to the wolf and its nature of ferocity as a huntress. They were perhaps taken as a signifier for unbridled forces of nature and those that ruled unregulated within nature. Those whose dread and veneration were, by equal share, felt and held by Vedic society. The Krittikas could also be linked with the goddesses in the Hindu pantheon, namely Durga and Kali, who are themselves portrayed as powerful and awe-inspiring protector goddesses of nature.

The likelihood that the Krittikas might have been an influence upon or influenced by subsequent European accounts of the Cynocephali is an appealing one. Possibly proposing that mythological concepts and imagery might have traveled along ancient trade routes and networks of cultural exchange. This is due to the fact that Indian mythology and culture had a deep influence on many ancient cultures. Cultures such as the Romans and Greeks, and they too had an influence on it.

Why do humans find the dog-headed creatures, across cultures and centuries, such an attraction? One reason lies in the symbolic role of predators, wolves and dogs in particular, which uneasily occupy the human psyche. Both feared and admired, they are the exemplars of paradoxes of protector and destroyer, life and death. As guardians and hunters, they have always been valued for being clever, loyal, and fierce, but feared for their ability to wound and master what is around them.

The Dogman, a man with a dog's head, is the traditional image of the symbolic power involved. His presence in so many disparate cultures is a testament to a ubiquity of richness and of interest in the liminal. Something or someone that lives in worlds as both human and beast. This is a concept that belongs to the Dogman, because there are other creatures, such as the Centaur and the Minotaur, that belong to this interstitial category. The Minotaur, for instance, with a human torso and bull legs, is the war between human and beast. Whereas the Centaur, human torso and horse below, is the union of sense and brute force.

The hypothesis that myths might contain recollections of vanished species or mangled observations is another intriguing one. Might stories about dog-headed people be based on real observation of unusual species or hybrids? The possibility in the absence of certain proof these myths are based on true events or contact with beings outside of categories is a captivating notion. The human mind is set up to understand patterns and to get the world to make sense. And one might expect that ancient civilizations might have seen foreign or strange creatures like dog-headed people. Then, taking these experiences and fitting them into their myths and legends.

In the end, the origin of the Dogman and his possible descendants will remain to be a complicated and diverse projection. A projection of both the symbolic power of a predator and the human perception of the unknown. Whether they spring from religious symbolism or actual events, the many accounts of dog-headed creatures throughout history are evidence of an integral feature of the human condition. It is our need to explore the boundary, and our continued striving to comprehend and make sense of the world that surrounds us.

CHAPTER 2
NOTABLE MODERN-DAY SIGHTINGS

Myth and legend may taint our current vision about mysterious monsters, but they are not of the past. Even now, credible people are reporting terrifying visions of explanation-defying sightings. Tales of bi-pedal wolf-like creatures, the Dogman, and other cryptids. Creatures who do not sit solely in the realm of old myth. They're still told, in hushed tones, and shrieked in terror. They stretch across decades, repeating and repeating, as if something just out of our reach continues and refuses to fade into myth.

Witnesses talk of intelligent beasts with terrifying eyes that glow like embers. Standing at immense heights, and jaws full of sharp, protruding fangs. They talk of them creeping along the borders of fields, crouching in the dark woods, staring from the shadows. They talk of them on lonely roads, of a horror coming into existence only to be lost in the shadows. Wherever it is, between America's green ridges or Europe's dark forests, such encounters rouse something deep within us—fear, awe, perhaps even recognition.

The debate continues as skeptics call for evidence while the faithful claim the truth already exists. A truth found in footprints, foreboding cries, and testimony of fearfulness from those adamant they witnessed what could not exist. This is not about monsters at all but about all of us. And what we do not understand links to something within us and pulls on the delicate threads of what we believe is the true world. When we attempt to delve into things left unknown, we're definitely not searching just for beasts to slay, we may get answers about ourselves.

THE GABLE FILM

The *Gable Film* first emerged on the internet in 2007, evoking widespread interest and debate from cryptozoologists, skeptics, and horror movie enthusiasts in alike. It was first introduced as a series of old 8mm home movies purportedly shot in the late 1970s.

The clip felt like a genuine, unedited recording of everyday life filmed by a cameraman, whose identity was not disclosed. Then there appears someone riding on a snowmobile in the winter landscape, a man chopping firewood in the woods, and a group of people taking part in outdoor activity. The grainy, low-quality texture of the footage and the amateur style of the cameraman helped create the documentary-like aesthetic of the film. This lent to the look of an authentic, never-before-seen glimpse into the past.

As the video went on, the tone of the film dramatically changed from ordinary to foreboding. In the last scene of the film, an unidentified creature abruptly appears, running towards the camera with deadly ferocity. The creature pounces and kills the cameraman after a brief pursuit. The sudden appearance of the creature was followed by a tremendous impact. There is a second part of the movie that appears to be a police investigation. During which time, the body of the cameraman is then discovered, half of which has vanished, apparently being devoured by the monster.

The abrupt break at the film's conclusion only made the mystery deeper, with more questions than could be answered many times over. Just the creepy nature of the clip, coupled with the clearly deteriorated state of the film and dissolved image, added to the reality that made speculations of its origin easier. The fact that it was used as found footage made the film realistic as well. This is a format that had already been popularized by the success of films like *The Blair Witch Project* (1999). The suspenseful atmosphere, and that the film looked old and of poor quality, made individuals believe it was a real, unreleased, straight-from-the-time footage.

Since its initial appearance, the *Gable Film* started an entire world of theories that all attempted to clarify the strange film footage. Most of these theories fell into three groups, each possessing some worldview about what the film actually was and had captured.

The cryptozoologists were quick to claim that the *Gable Film* was proof of the Michigan Dogman. The legendary creature which has the head of a dog and the body of a man. This account theorized that the film was real historical footage documenting an experience with the beast. Maintaining that the movie provided tangible evidence of an enduring beast of regional folklore. With many arguing to support this explanation that the low-quality, grainy nature of the footage provided evidence for it being genuine. With many observers theorizing, the film had been shot many years previously, indeed even in the 1970s, as claimed. In order to generate speculation about the beast's nature and origin, they drew attention to the fact that it seemed so unearthly, as though by reason beyond human comprehension.

Others argued that this was possibly some proof of otherworldly involvement. They also theorized the monster was not a biological entity at all, maybe something interdimensional, or ghostlike, but then perhaps an extraterrestrial alien too. That is, according to normal werewolf, skinwalker, or shape-shifter mythologies. This theory held that the *Gable Film* was not a victory over a monstrosity of the flesh but an appeal to supernatural power or energy. This was supported by the supernatural atmosphere of the film. Combined with the apparently impossible actions of the creature as they were construed to go against nature and the laws of physics.

But most skeptics watched the video and found anomalies that exposed it as a hoax. Some pointed to the fact that the "monster" was moving in a way that was uncharacteristic for animals. Its posture and gait were awkward and unnatural. Some argued that the film's deterioration seemed staged, pointing towards digital tampering instead of an organic process. The skeptics exposed the film as a carefully crafted hoax, one intended to make people believe what was not there. They used the chronologically misplaced features of the film, including the use of contemporary camera technology and editing processes to produce the images, as a proof of its deliberate creation. As the controversy over the *Gable Film* raged, the doubters were vocal in their assertions. They contended that the film's authenticity was strongly suspected, and that its nature was most probably that of a skillfully constructed piece of fiction.

Then in 2010 all that was revealed concerning the film. The *Gable Film* was proven once and for all to be a fraud, ending all the controversy and intrigue surrounding it. This was revealed by MonsterQuest, the investigation television show. MonsterQuest was a History Channel series between 2007-2010, which examined well-known sightings or experiences of several supernatural beasts. The program spent an entire episode examining the footage and revealing the truth behind where it was shot. In the investigation's course, it was revealed that the film had been made on purpose by Mike Agrusa. Agrusa is a Michigan-born man who was very passionate about cryptid history and enjoys spinning tales.

Agrusa, a superb director and special effects technician, had produced the film with current equipment and special effects techniques aimed at making it look like it was old footage. Agrusa really did film it with an 8mm camera. This created a sense of age in the film, so people would believe the film was made years earlier than it actually was. The cinematic trick proved to be so effective that it had deceived even the most skeptical audience. This provoked widespread speculation about whether or not the film was genuine, along with the monster it depicted. A series of key factors contributed to the debunking of the film, each providing an important clue that pointed towards its make-believe nature.

Agrusa told them the "creature" from the movie was actually a man dressed in a ghillie suit. This type of suit is used by hunters and military snipers to disguise themselves. This information not only explained the strange appearance of the creature but also called into question the production quality of the movie. It appeared there was a substantial amount of planning that went into it. Using a ghillie suit, a comparatively unusual and specialized piece of equipment showed that Agrusa had a significant number of resources available to him and the know-how to use them. This was just further evidence in favor that the film was a willful hoax. Film and video analysts showed that the film's aging effects were unreal and didn't correlate with the common degradation of film.

Rather, they seemed to have been artificially inserted by the application of digital filters and post-processing. This was impressive in itself. It implied that Agrusa had taken the trouble to create a sense of age and deterioration in a bid to make the film appear more realistic. Application of digital filtering and post-processing was an unmistakable sign that the movie had been tampered with, and not a genuine, raw record of history.

While the film was thought initially to be from the 1970s, inspection of its format, use of camera, and staging told a different story. It was clearly a contemporary effort made to appear old. This mismatch was a big red flag, as it showed that the film had been deliberately made to mislead viewers and provide a false impression of history. Using the new camera technology and post-production methods, along with the chronological errors in the movie, it was sure that the *Gable Film* was indeed a 21st-century film, and not an actual past recording.

Even though it was established beyond a shadow of doubt to be a hoax, the *Gable Film* left a lasting impact on cryptozoology and urban legend fandom. The film generated additional interest in the Michigan Dogman, which had originally been seen in 1887. However, it became extremely popular after the release of *The Legend*, a 1987 song by Michigan disc jockey Steve Cook.

The *Gable Film* also helped to fuel the popularity of "found footage" type horror, as independent filmmakers created their own such films. Even when the film had been revealed as a hoax, it was still a widely popular reference point in debates about the evidence for cryptids and hoaxes. Such hoaxes are perhaps fun but detract from the researchers who are working hard to provide good and verifiable evidence.

THE SIEGE OF LOCKETT RANCH

The Siege of Lockett Ranch stands as the most chilling and frightening of all the ever-reported Dogman sightings. Happening in Taylor, Mississippi, back in 1948, the foreboding story has been covered in-depth in a variety of mediums. Everything from videos and audio shows to books and online discussion boards. The central figure of this eerie saga, Edward Lockett III. He is remarkably still alive today, as of the writing of this book, serving as a living witness to the horrors that befell his family.

The family was one of the first settlers in the area going back to 1832 when Taylor, Mississippi, was founded. Edward Lockett, Sr. purchased the property from the Chickasaw tribe and had lived on it for many years. Throughout this time, all was well and quiet. Then in 1948 things took a different turn for the Lockett family after Edward Sr. signed a contract with a local sawmill for them to timber part of the property.

Edward Lockett III was only a child of 12 years at that time. He recalls for us that his family had lived on the ranch for generations. His grandfather, Edward Lockett Sr., had constructed the ranch himself, striving to give the family a secure and successful future. But despite the ranch's history and the family's firm foundation, something evil was brewing in the surrounding woods.

The logging crew had spent several weeks clearing a roadway to the far end on the property. This section of their land was reported to be sacred to the Chickasaw tribe. The following week, full-scale logging of the property was under way. This is when things first began to get a little strange.

With easier access to the backside of the property, Edward Lockett, Sr. and his friend ventured there to hunt and trap. It seems they had come across several severed deer heads with no remains of the bodies being present. The unusual aspect is that one of the heads was placed on top of a stick that was stuck straight up into the ground. They had the impression this was some type of warning.

It wasn't long after this when the logging crew came out of the woods in a panic. It seems one of the crew members disappeared and the only remains they found was his bloody shirt. These were hardened woodsmen who were now shaken to the core. After searching for the missing man, everyone spoke in hushed tones and was on edge. They knew they had seen something out there, but what?

The Lockett family encounter started as a string of unexplainable occurrences that grew darker and more sinister in nature. What began initially was strange noises during the middle of the night and later escalated into attacks by mysterious creatures described as dogmen. The creature, with its unsettling hybrid form, brought an overwhelming sense of terror into the Lockett home.

At first, there were only minor events, but soon enough, the whole Lockett ranch was on edge. Chickens and hogs would just disappear, leaving behind nothing but the sweet smell of moist soil and the unsettling feeling of the unknown. Crops were ruined, their stalks broken like dry twigs, and the family attributed these to the activities of wild animals like wolves and bears. They even thought maybe it was a hungry beggar scavenging for food and leftovers from the fields.

But it worsened with time. The mutilated bodies of the cattle and the household dogs were discovered in a manner impossible for any common animal to do. They were disemboweled with precision, as if by some intelligent being, and their bones crushed as if smashed by some heavy force. It was as if the creature had an advanced knowledge of anatomy, slowly peeling flesh from bone without leaving behind even a shred of evidence. The family's darkest fears were realized when they found the body of a cow, its skin ripped open in a horrific display of brutality. The memory was seared into their minds as furiously as an iron, indelibly imprinting itself on their shared psyche.

And then the howling began. It wasn't wolf howls; there was something much more unnatural in the sound of them. Something that crawled the spines of everyone who ever heard them. Guttural, deep and dreadfully human-like. The noise woke the Lockett's with a start instantly. The noises seemed to originate from everywhere all at once, as if the very forest itself were in torment. They would be awakened during the night, ears perked up, attempting to hear and locate where the wailing was coming from. But the howls seemed to come from every direction and no direction at all. The incessant howling was continually reminding them they were not working with a clear animal brutality. The Locketts were captive in their own home, bound by the darkness that inched just outside the edge of the forest. They knew they had to do something, but they did not know what, or how, to battle the evil that had invaded their land.

One evening, while Edward Sr. rode out across the ranch carrying his rifle on patrol, he got his first good look at the creature.

Partially concealed in the dying light of day, standing in the shadows of the tree line, was a bi-pedal half-man, half-wolf creature. It had a muscular body with grayish fur that seemed to absorb the fading light. It stood about seven feet tall and was nearly invisible in those conditions. Its eyes seemed to flash red in the darkness and this sent a chill down Edward's spine, and its sharp, wolf-like muzzle appeared to curl into a horrifying grin. The eyes glowed with a fierce inner flame, lighting the surrounding darkness. The creature's eyes did not blink, their stares being hard and piercing, as though they could look to the very core of Edward's being.

The beast stood stock still for what seemed like an eternity, its overwhelming presence occupying the entire clearing. Edward's breath hitched inside his throat as he fought to understand what he was being shown. His eyes were drinking in something, but his brain refused to let him accept something he knew that could never, ever be. The monster looking there as though it was constructed of his worst nightmare, a human walking incarnation of horror living within the shadows of the forest. And yet, despite all the terror that was surrounding him, Edward was paralyzed with fear and could not avert his gaze. It was as if he was drawn to the beast by an irresistible force, like a moth to a fire. At last, after what seemed like an eternity to Edward, the beast disappeared into the forest.

From then on, the Dogmen grew braver, making themselves more and more apparent. Shadows darted rapidly between the trees, and glowing eyes peered out of the gloom. The creatures seemed to possess intelligence, as they had seemed to observe the family like they were patterning them. They came and went in a flash, their timing always when tensions were most strained, or fears most keen. The family became paranoid and thought the Dogmen were making them crazy, creating visions and sounds for them to see and hear by manipulating their fears and imagination. They would wake up in the middle of the night knowing that they could hear someone pacing back and forth outside their window. Then only later to discover that the noise was merely wind blowing through the trees. And despite all the suspicion that had surrounded them, the family knew that they were not alone on the ranch. They knew the Dogman was always near, waiting, watching to see what they would do next.

The all-out attack on Lockett Ranch started on a night when the moon was not visible in the autumn of 1948. The bi-pedal beasts came out of the darkness, their snarls ringing in the quiet air. They scratched at the windows and doors, trying to get in. The family defended themselves frantically with rifles and shotguns, taking potshots at the beasts through openings in the wooden barriers they had quickly set up over the doors and windows.

The fight continued for hours. Bullets barely slowed the Dogmen down and they were not fatal to them. The outside walls of the house were covered with deep scratches where claws had scoured them, and several windows were broken. Edward Sr. was able to injure one of the Dogmen one time by shooting it in the eye. He saw it emit a blood-curdling scream before it disappeared back into the woods. But their triumph was short-lived since the creatures would come again, more ferocious and fiercer than ever.

At dawn, the creatures retreated at last, and a ruined ranch was left behind. The cattle had almost been eradicated, and the once great homestead was now a battle-scarred zone. The Locketts realized they would not survive another night of attacks. It was at this point that the family made the tough decision to leave their house.

Sadly, the Locketts were wrong to think they had finally freed themselves from the terrifying creatures that had been tearing up their property. They packed everything they could and raced to the closest town for safety, leaving the ranch as a last resort. But their ordeal was only beginning. The Dogmen, apparently, pursued the family relentlessly and did not stay on the ranch. They stalked, pursuing the Locketts down the roads that took them further away from home, leaving a path of destruction and fear behind them.

The Lockett's best chance was to come up with a way to outsmart their pursuers and escape the claws of the dark creatures that had already ended some lives. But glancing over their shoulders, they couldn't help feeling that they were being followed and that the creatures were at their heels. It is here that Edward Sr. had planned to sell off half of the property so that he could strengthen their original home for a shootout with these creatures.

Edward Sr. resolved that they had no other option but to tackle the menace once and for all. He had locked up the house, and he assembled a number of men from the town who were carrying weapons. He created a hunting party to regain the family ranch. This included war veterans and experienced hunters who then set off into the forest with a determination to end the terror.

As they moved further into the thick forest, the hunting party stood at the boundary of a clearing that appeared to be imbued with a dark and ominous power. The atmosphere was thick with a sort of preternatural presence, and the trees appeared to twist and writhe in the dying light of day. It was as though the forest itself was cautioning them, telling them, go back, turn away from the secrets that the forest held in its womb. But the hunters, with fear and wanton curiosity propelling them, disregarded the warning, their chests thudding with their hearts.

And then they noticed huge nest-like formations. Edward's party progressed slowly, their gaze at the emptiness inside. Looking into the darkness, they were greeted by a view that froze them to their very core. Bones covered the ground, both animal and human, a grim reminder of some long past and forgotten tragedy. The air was heavy with the smell of rot, and they carried the burden of history on their shoulders.

The Dogmen attacked once again with a fury unmatched as they sensed the Lockett's desperation. The air was electric with tension as the family prepared for a final showdown with the creatures that had hunted them for so long. This night was dark and foreboding, the only sound the distant hum of crickets and the creaking of trees in the wind. But as the Dogmen burst forth from the shadows, the silence was shattered by the roar of gunfire.

The fight continued on; the Locketts struggled to hold on as the creatures encircled them. Edward Sr. held his ground, firing his rifle over and over to drive the hordes of monsters away. His friends and family members fought together, firing their rifles in short, managed bursts to kill the creatures one at a time. Despite all their efforts, the Dogmen just wouldn't quit. Their numbers appeared to be never-ending as they poured out of the forest's edge.

The night fell into a whirlpool of devastation and chaos. Gunfire could be heard ringing out among the trees as the Locketts fought for their lives. Bullets flew through the air, with most missing their desired targets while striking trees and rocks with precision. However, the Dogmen made an impact as their claws and teeth tore through the house with a cruel savagery. Cries of horror from the family mixed with the gunfire created sounds that seemed to shake the earth to its very core.

As the fight continued, the Locketts grew weary. They were outgunned and outnumbered by the sheer ferocity of these creatures. Edward Sr. realized that they could not continue this much longer, that at some point they would be overpowered by sheer numbers of the Dogmen. Edward Sr. was feeding a cold fury in himself, a fury that would consume him entirely. He repeatedly fired his rifle. The bullets ripping into the monsters with deadly accuracy. But even as he battled, he realized that it was too late. The monsters had won, and the Locketts had lost. The family abandoned Taylor, Mississippi, moving some fifty miles away, though Edward Lockett III would return many years later as an adult to learn more about where he came from.

The events surrounding the Siege of Lockett Ranch have been well documented, drawing people in through podcasts, books, and internet forums. Paranormal investigators still dispute the accuracy of the encounter, with some regarding it as being one of the strongest cases of Dogmen encounters in recent history.

The ruins of the former ranch serve as an ominous reminder of the horrors the Lockett family endured there. As a terrifying reminder that the Dogmen are not entirely gone, some locals still say that on certain nights, the howling of the creatures can be heard in the distance.

The Siege of Lockett Ranch is among the most frightening Dogman encounters ever. One may or may not believe in the Dogman and that's okay. But the tale of survival, fear, and mystery of the Lockett family battling them is a riveting narrative of survival that will keep us enthralled.

THE BEAST OF BRAY ROAD

Of all the hundreds of cryptid myths plaguing North America, perhaps one of the most frightening and well-documented is the Beast of Bray Road. A werewolf type spooky beast, the mysterious creature, has allegedly harassed residents of Elkhorn, Wisconsin, for centuries. In contrast to some of the anecdotal-only cryptid myths, the Beast of Bray Road has been supported by a vast number of eyewitness accounts, newspaper articles, and actual investigative work. Its popularity has grown significantly since the second half of the 20th century, and its legend is compared to other bi-pedal dog-like cryptids such as the Michigan Dogman.

Most people mistakenly believe the Bray Road sightings started in Elkhorn, Wisconsin, in the late 1980s and early 1990s. That is not true with the very first non-indigenous Dogman type creature sighting being in 1936. It began with Mark Shackleman, who was employed by the St. Coletta School for Exceptional Children. The school was in Jefferson, which is only a brief thirty miles straight as the crow flies away from Elkhorn. This is the one that really began it all.

Mark Shackleman drove into St. Coletta School for Exceptional Children at midnight, the darkness of the rural night enveloping him like a shroud. He was the school's night watchman, and he patrolled these grounds nightly. As he walked, he would hear his footfalls echoing off the ancient buildings and disturbing the leaves of the orchard. The school stood in a closed Franciscan convent just beyond the quiet town of Jefferson. Its grounds were a broad arc of rolling hills, open fields and wide vistas. It also had centuries-old Native American burial grounds that had been left intact for generations. He wore a reliable flashlight on his hip, its beam cutting through the darkness like a pillar of self-assurance.

The year was 1936, and Mark was in his thirties, a husband and father who worked the uneventful job for a paycheck to support his family. In rural Jefferson, there wasn't much to worry about, except the occasional burglar or some rowdy teenagers playing a prank. But tonight, things felt different. As Mark trudged around his patrol route, the moon created long ominous shadows over the grounds. Then he saw a dark silhouette hunched over one of the old burial mounds. The creature's canine form looked like it dug with a fierceness that bordered on well, human intensity. Its claws scraped against the earth, dirt and small rocks scattering everywhere, and its labored breathing was the sole noise to penetrate the silence of the darkness.

Mark's eyes narrowed as he tried to make out what the creature was. From the canine way it dug, it could have been a dog or maybe a wolf. But even from far away, Mark could see that the thing was far too big for that. Its body seemed to tug at the ground as if it were attempting to excavate something that was buried deep in the mound. Mark's heart started racing inside his chest when he understood the creature wasn't excavating something; somehow, it was searching for something. Then, suddenly, it froze and looked upwards, its eyes fixed on Mark in an unyielding stare. The body of the beast braced itself. Its muscles tensed beneath its thick fur, and for one moment Mark forgot to breathe or move, caught fast in a state of paralysis.

And then, in a flash of movement, the creature stood up, its sleek, hairy body unfurling to over six feet tall. Its shaggy canine face was twisted into a snarl, its teeth bared, and its lips pulled back in a sinister smile. Mark could see a small glint of fangs in the moonlight. His heart suddenly missed a beat as he understood that this was not a common animal. The body of this creature was muscle-bound and gigantic. Mark's mind went blank as he attempted to comprehend what he was witnessing, his brain struggling to grasp the impossible.

Instantly, without warning, there was the low rumble of a growl on the other side of the field, and Mark's back bristled with fear. He caught the stench of rotting flesh; an odor so rank that it clung to the beast's coat like a shroud. His heart thundering in his chest, forcing himself to breathe slowly, Mark retreated, his eyes on the creature. In a flash of ferocity, the creature wheeled around and bolted off into the forest, disappearing into the blackness like a phantom. Mark was left alone in the field, his thoughts racing with the consequences of what he had just witnessed.

The following night, Mark went back to St. Coletta for his rounds, flashlight in hand. Walking the grounds, he spotted the shadow again, digging into the same hill as the previous night. This time, he held his flashlight firmly, prepared to run or swing if necessary. The creature rose, its eyes fixed on Mark unblinking, and Mark saw the flash of fangs in the moonlight. But this time, the creature opened its mouth, showing rows of teeth that were razor sharp. Mark saw the fangs dangling below the other teeth, and its lips curled into a snarl. The air was thick with tension as the creature growled at Mark. It seemed to speak in some kind of half-human and half-beast sounds. Mark's heart pounded in his chest while his brain was telling him to run, but his legs were not obeying. He was frozen to the spot. A mere victim of the stare emanating from the beast that seemed to penetrate his soul.

The growl from the creature seemed to be a warning, a sign that it should not be disobeyed. He stood still, and the creature disappeared for the second time. He never again saw the thing, but the monstrous growl, the fact that it was actually speaking to him, lasted for years.

While reports of a strange bi-pedal wolf-like animal in Wisconsin might pre-date its mainstream fame, the legend of the Beast of Bray Road itself caught on in the late 1980s. The first widely reported sighting was in 1989 when local resident Lori Endrizzi reported having a frightening encounter with a muscular creature while driving along Bray Road. She recalled seeing a large, hairy monster with pointed ears, long claws, and red eyes at dusk, as if it seemed to be feeding on roadkill. She was slowing down to get a better view when the creature looked in her direction, cruelly glaring before she drove away frightened.

Soon after Endrizzi's experience, others in Elkhorn came forward with similar chilling accounts. Some saw a similar creature off in the distance, while others said they were pursued or stalked by something that had an uncanny, unearthly presence. According to reports, these sightings happened on roads adjoining forested areas, at the edge of town, and on the isolated stretches of Bray Road. This added an otherworldly quality of desolation to the experience.

The Beast of Bray Road may have remained merely another lost small-town legend but for the relentless reporting of Linda Godfrey. She was working for a small-town paper, The Week, and Godfrey at first briefly dismissed the tales. Later, however, after she heard more of them, she immediately realized that there were too many witnesses telling reasonably similar things. That made it impossible to write off the story. It was as if the stories of a ghost animal were not myths, but a communal remembrance of a common experience.

She began documenting the sightings, interviewing witnesses who had nothing to gain by making up such sightings. She was struck by the uniformity of the descriptions: a big, two-legged dog with black fur , glowing eyes that cut through the darkness. The creature could move with unmatchable speed and agility, as if it had originated from another world. The witnesses approximate the Beast to be some seven feet tall, heavily built and almost supernatural. They told of its eyes, glowing with an unearthly amber gleam, and how it melted into the darkness like a ghost.

As Godfrey continued to research the story, she discovered a trend in the sightings. The creature was seen late at night, on highways and side roads. Witnesses reported it to run alongside their cars, driving them crazy with fear. Some of the witnesses only got quick glimpses of it, others got glances from afar, but all of them experienced the same fear and horror at seeing this preternatural apparition.

All of Godfrey's investigative work culminated not just in the newspaper stories, but also in the publication of multiple books. The most notable of these is *The Beast of Bray Road: Tailing Wisconsin's Werewolf,* which helped solidify this cryptid's place in modern folklore. Her research not only shed light on the legend of the Beast of Bray Road, but it also sparked a nationwide conversation about the existence of unknown bi-pedal creatures.

One of the most compelling aspects of the Beast of Bray Road myth is the sheer amount of eyewitness accounts. Each describes in lavish detail some strange animal that cannot be explained. Probably, the most publicity-craving account was likely the teenager who was called to testify that he saw the Beast on its hind legs in his backyard during the 1990s. The teenager supposedly was frozen in terror as the seven-foot beast, in his opinion, stared at him through a window with an unblinking gaze. The

Beast supposedly let out a low, growling noise that ran through his body and vanished into the night, leaving him upset and shaken.

And then in 1991, a local farmer arrived with a terrifying account of his meeting with the Beast. He recounts how he had seen a huge wolf-like animal along a fence on his farm, with wide shoulders and a muscular build that radiated intelligence and menace. The farmer recalled the creature's eyes, which gleamed with an eerie light and the snarling smile, which seemed to be a mouthful of wild anger. He couldn't help but feel nervous since the monster was more than simply a savage beast; it was something with a strong will and an innate awareness of its surroundings.

An overnight driver on one night in 1992 also had a similar hair-raising experience with the Beast. He claimed he saw an abnormal creature bound across the road in one leap, the speed of which was ghostly quiet and abnormal. When he pulled over to examine it closer, he could hear the heavy breathing and sounds of rustling leaves in the bushes by his side that made his skin crawl. The driver described the sound as a rumble he had never experienced in his entire life, a rasping growling noise that appeared to emanate deep within the beast itself. Such descriptions, and dozens more like them, point to a chain of events that give substance to the theory that there is indeed something appallingly wrong. Something terrorizing the countryside, sowing fear and wonder in its wake.

To this day, the Beast of Bray Road sightings have not stopped, and new witnesses step forward to describe their experiences and interactions with this elusive creature. Years pass, but the legend is not forgotten, and its mystique remains to tantalize the public as much as entice a new wave of cryptozoologists and paranormal investigators. The event has also succeeded with the media, as new TV specials, documentaries, and even horror films attempt to make the tale mainstream.

One of the most popularly accepted is the 2005 movie *The Beast of Bray Road*, produced solely to make the legend popular and mainstream. While the movie did not become a box office hit, it further solidified the beast into contemporary culture and brought the legend to a new generation of people and believers. Paranormal investigators and YouTube cryptozoologists make the pilgrimage to the site today, attempting to uncover proof of the Beast's existence. Armed with camcorders, tape machines, and a healthy sense of skepticism, these contemporary treasure hunters search the Wisconsin woods and highways for any sign of the elusive beast.

The extended life of the Beast of Bray Road is a testament to folklore and human imagination. Whatever it is, whether some actual cryptid, an enormous hoax, or some middle ground of misidentification and folklore, it is one of the longest running legends in American cryptozoology. No matter what the day-by-day headlines say and the ongoing curiosity, the Beast remains a mystery. But there also remains one lingering question: Does it even exist? Is there a bi-pedal monster that haunts this Wisconsin's road? Only time and ongoing study will reveal the truth. And while the hunt continues, have no doubt, the Beast of Bray Road will be an American legend. One that will forever hold the hearts and minds of those courageous enough to think the unthinkable.

THE LAND BETWEEN THE LAKES (LBL) MASSACRE

The Land Between the Lakes National Recreation Area was originally a 1960s project. This is when the Tennessee Valley Authority (TVA) began buying 170,000 acres between Kentucky Lake and Lake Barkley in a plan to construct the recreation area. The megaproject was intended for 10 million yearly visitors as part of a broader initiative by President John F. Kennedy and Secretary of the Interior Stuart Udall. This initiative was to construct National Recreation Areas across the country. The property was developed in a multi-purpose style, with amenities including a bison range, and included the building of a dam across the Cumberland River to form Lake Barkley. They then added a canal linking the two lakes, which was finished in 1964.

The area was legislated as a national recreation area by President Kennedy in 1963 and had development money available during the administration of President Johnson. Development was not without sacrifice, however, as 103,000 acres were bought out and roughly 2,700 people were moved from 900 Tennessee and Kentucky households. A majority of the community's residents fiercely resisted relocation and loss of their rural way of life. This was the second move for many of these families because of the construction of the Kentucky Dam from 1938 to 1944.

During the 1990s, the TVA redirected its operations away from directly subsidized taxpayer-funded operations. Then in 1998, the US Congress approved the transfer of operations in the area to the United States Department of Agriculture's U.S. Forest Service.

The Land Between the Lakes (LBL) is a wide and peaceful land along the west borders of Kentucky and Tennessee. It is a land so wonderfully beautiful that it has attracted many individuals to the center. This magical area, where the rolling hills of the Appalachian foothills blend with the peaceful waters of Lake Barkley and Kentucky Lake, is a haven for wildlife, outdoor enthusiasts. It also draws those who love solitude in nature. The varied terrain of the LBL, with its steep forests, rolling hills, and meandering streams, offers a pristine haven for a diverse array of plant and animal life. So much so that the area seems like heaven for nature enthusiasts and photographers alike.

But to the brave few who see beyond its peaceful veneer, LBL also holds a secret. A secret that is far more sinister than one would imagine. Rumored whispers have it as the hideout of a monster. Some are afraid of this beast, which some say perpetrated one of the most horrific events ever attributed to a cryptid: the LBL

Dogman Massacre. This creature is commonly referred to as the LBL Dogman within the community. It is reported to be a hybrid creature that uses the physical form of a dog, the speed and ferocity of a wolf, and the shape of a human torso. Its presence has been surrounded by speculation, with some claiming to have seen it in the forest, while others have spoken of hearing its haunting howls during the night.

A camping trip by a four-member family became a horror show when the family was assaulted by a bizarre and grotesque creature in the Land Between the Lakes (LBL) woods. The camp was destroyed, and their bodies were discovered mutilated and scattered without. Their camper showed no signs of a break in. The assault was not typical due to the sheer brutality of it. And no evidence was found of the creature devouring the dead corpses as a source of sustenance. This suggested some kind of intelligence and tactical conduct that goes beyond any normal wild animal behavior.

This is a rendition of the account by Jan Thompson. Jan worked the night shift at a nearby convenience store and was the first to go public with what took place.

I was not part of the investigation but overheard and eventually joined the conversation between the deputy sheriffs who were directly involved with the incident. They had just returned from the crime scene in the Land Between the Lakes area where they had worked for over 8 hours. They arrived at the gas station approximately at 3:00 a.m. hoping to forget what they had witnessed.

Both officers, Adam and Bill, were traumatized to the core. There was a mix of fear, confusion, shock, and disbelief emanating from both of them. Adam's face was as white as chalk, and he sat on the curb, head between his knees, vomiting the rest of what was remaining in his stomach. Bill, however, was visibly shaken, with wide bloodshot eyes, and what seemed to be a deep-seated fear.

I stood outside the gas station, thinking I could help them, and I offered Adam Rolaids to calm his stomach. Crickets singing, buzzing flies, and the hum of highway traffic in the distance were the only sounds to be heard. My head was spinning as I wondered what in the world could have shaken them so badly. Maybe it was a deadly car accident, a murder, or even a dead body was found.

After sitting in stunned silence for approximately 15 minutes, they finally started speaking to each other. Adam started first. His words were only a whisper. "I just can't believe it...it's impossible. I just can't believe it," Bill agreed, speaking as quietly as Adam had. "I know.it was...is...it is so unbelievable. I've never seen anything like this."

When they recounted their experience, I invited them in and sat down with them. I was captivated with every sentence while listening to them talk. They were called out to investigate a scene at one of LBL's isolated camps. It was around sunset when they arrived, and not long after that, they were confronted with an unthinkable horror. Another couple came upon the scene and had already phoned the police. The victims were a family, a father, a mother, a son, and a small daughter who had been brutally murdered.

The officers were horrified by what they saw. The victims' bodies were mutilated, with deep claw marks and bite wounds that seemed to be from an unknown animal. Even the coroner was baffled, unable to determine the cause of death. The officers were convinced that a bear was responsible, but as they continued to investigate, they discovered evidence that suggested otherwise.

A dress belonging to a small girl was found in the motor home, leading the officers to believe that a child was missing. A search party was formed, and after 7 hours, the missing child was found hanging from a tree branch, her body mutilated and partially eaten. The officers were devastated, and their lives were forever changed.

As I sat with Adam and Bill, I couldn't help but feel a sense of unease. Their story was one of unimaginable horror, and I couldn't shake the feeling that something was watching us, waiting for its next victim.

Months later, Adam and Bill returned to the gas station, their faces showing worry and stress. They had received news about the lab tests taken from the crime scene, and the results were astonishing. They tested the saliva taken from the bite marks and the hair found on the victim's fingers and in the tree. The lab stated they were from an unknown species but similar to a Canis Lupis, or wolf.

In the aftermath, official reports of the incident were mysteriously absent. Some who lived near LBL at the time recalled hearing about the attack only through whispers. Law enforcement and park officials either denied the event entirely or claimed that a bear had been responsible, a convenient explanation for an unexplainable horror.

However, certain local officials and even a few of the park rangers have reportedly come forward over the years after retiring with cryptid acknowledgments. One former ranger allegedly admitted that he had been called to the scene and had witnessed nothing like it before or since. The way the bodies had been torn apart, the sheer destruction of the RV. The apparent precision of the attack led him to believe they were dealing with something unnatural.

Believers argue that a cover-up was enacted to prevent mass panic and to protect the thriving tourism industry in LBL. If the general public knew that an unclassified predator roamed these woods, would they ever return?

Aside from the famous 1982 encounter, there are many reports of the Dogman of LBL which exist and are widespread. Campers, hunters, and hikers alike have reported sightings of a gigantic, bipedal wolf-like creature which leaves an overbearing feeling of fear and foreboding. Each of them describes having the feeling and presence of being watched, hearing horrific growling sounds at nighttime. Or of catching ghostly red or yellow colors observing them just behind the tree line.

One of the most spine-tingling reports is that of a hunter in the late 1990s. The hunter claims to have shot at the animal point-blank, only to have it unleash a thunderous roar and vanish into the woods. Returning the next day to the site, he discovered no sign of blood, but rather giant dog-like footprints with deep claw marks on the ground.

Paranormal investigators and cryptid hunters have flocked to LBL in recent years, hoping to get a glimpse of the creature or evidence of its presence. A few have been able to get unexplained howls on tape, while others have reported observing dark mysterious figures running between trees.

The Land Between the Lakes remains America's most bizarre and unsettling destinations for unsuspecting visitors. Whether the Dogman is an unknown species, an extraterrestrial being, or just a vile rumor, one thing is certain: its horror is real. To its witnesses, there can be no denying there is an unnatural beast prowling the woods. The 1982 tragedy is still clouded in secrecy, and many questions are left unresolved. It is a vivid reminder of the evil terror that lies beyond the liminal edge.

There are many other reports of Dogman and Bigfoot sightings in this region. To those who are willing to risk it and venture into LBL, be well advised. Legend says the Dogman observes, waits, and if the legends are true, it is always hungry.

CHAPTER 3
EXAMINING SIGHTINGS ACROSS NORTH AMERICA

For decades, the Dogman legend has captured the imagination of believers and non-believers, generating both furious debates and a deep interest. The bipedal Dogman, a canid-like cryptid, has been the central theme of scores of reports and sightings. Typically reported as being between six and seven feet tall, with burning amber-red eyes at night. Having a threatening posture that sends a shiver down the spine of those who claim to have glimpsed it. Skeptics attribute such visions as misidentifications, pranks, or psychological effects. But some insist the Dogman is a genuine, yet unknown species that prowl the forest, waiting to be discovered.

Dogman sightings have also been reported throughout much of North America, with some areas being hotspots for such sightings. From the heavy forests of the Pacific Northwest to the rural Midwest, and from the Appalachian area to the South's wetlands, these are among the top favorites for Dogman activity. A few of the most prominent places include Wisconsin's rural areas, where residents have described seeing the beast walking through woods and fields. We also have Michigan, where many have been spotted throughout the Upper Peninsula.

The Dogman's reported haunts are places with dense cover, broken country, and a general atmosphere of remoteness. Places like these are best suited to a creature surrounded by secrecy. It is not surprising that many people believe the Dogman is not so much a legend as a fact. There is no definitive proof to validate the creature's existence. The frequency of sightings and the consistency of the reports may prove there is more to the myth than meets the eye. As we move further along the path of Dogman sightings, it is clear this is a phenomenon that still mystifies and fascinates us today. A phenomenon that may yet hold the key to unlocking the mysteries of the unknown.

MICHIGAN

Michigan holds a special place in Dogman history. It is the location of some of the most frequently reported and oldest sightings of the elusive creature. The legend of the Michigan Dogman begins in 1887, when two lumberjacks in Wexford County saw something that could not be explained. A bi-pedal, half-dog, half-man beast with aspects that appeared to erase the boundary between the two. This marked the start of a prolonged and storied history of Dogman sightings in Michigan. Most of the sighting over the years have taken place across the Upper Peninsula and in northern Michigan's dense forests.

The Upper Peninsula, with its open spaces and sparse population, is frequently quoted as one of the most likely areas to find a dogman. The hilly terrain, dense forests, and plentiful wildlife provide the ideal setting for an elusive creature to thrive. It's easy to see why people would think the Dogman is real and not a myth. The mining and logging history of the region has also left behind a legacy of abandoned mines, old logging camps, and other remote areas. Areas that might offer the perfect type of habitat for this type of creature to live.

The Michigan Dogman legend went mainstream in 1987 when DJ Steve Cook dropped *The Legend,* a hit single about reported Dogman sightings. Cook had initially written the tune as an April Fool's prank, but listeners responded with their own chilling accounts. These calls just seemed to contribute to the impression that there was something sinister in Michigan's backcountry. The intoxicating melody and disquieting lyrics of the song appeared to access some reservoir of interest and fear that surrounded the legend of the Dogman. It was soon a cult classic among the people who are fans of the paranormal.

Michigan's dense woods, the heavy concentration of deer (a potential source of food), and open regions with sparse human population offer the ideal setting for a Dogman sighting. Michigan's vast tracts of wilderness, such as the Huron-Manistee National Forest and the Ottawa National Forest, offer an expansive and largely unmapped area for an animal to roam and hunt. The fact is most of these locations are isolated and inaccessible, which only serves to increase the mystique and mystery of the Dogman legend. This alone makes Michigan a hotspot of activity from those who claim to have sighted this bi-pedal legend.

WISCONSIN

Wisconsin also features a strange and interesting chapter in the history of Dogman Lore, as The Beast of Bray Road legend continues to intrigue people. This wolf-like, two-legged creature has been the subject of many reports and sightings, with most happening during the late 1980s and early 1990s. Elkhorn, a little town in the southeastern part of Wisconsin, was the center of these sightings. With most witnesses noting a creature which roamed the roads, pursued automobiles, and seemed to have some type of otherworldly intelligence about it.

This Dogman has been reported as a huge, wolf-like beast with a bi-pedal posture, with estimates ranging as high as 7 feet tall. The creature's eyes have been said to glow yellow/amber, its coat to be dirty and matted, and the way it moves to be slow and deliberate. Although it is reported as being enormous and has a foreboding posture, it is also said to be a sly and cunning creature. Many witness accounts claim that it can vanish into thin air or blend itself into the surrounding forests effortlessly.

Wisconsin's dense woods, farmland, and ribbon of rivers and caves offer the perfect terrain for an ominous large predator such as the Dogman. Wisconsin's rural landscape, composed of rolling hills, dense forests, and winding streams, gives the reclusive creature a vast unmapped territory to stalk and roam. There is also a large number of white-tailed deer in Wisconsin that would be a likely source of food for the Beast. This combination gives credibility to the possibility of it being a real and living danger to the area.

Other researchers have speculated that the Beast of Bray Road was not an isolated occurrence but one of the Dogman phenomena of sightings in the Midwest. This is evident in the fact that the creature has been seen elsewhere in the Midwest, including Michigan, Illinois, and even Texas. The possibility that they are relatives to each other, or to a greater kin population, raises compelling questions regarding the history and ways of the Dogman. This suggests the value of continued observation and investigation on this dubious but intriguing creature.

KENTUCKY & TENNESSEE

Along the border of Kentucky and Tennessee, Land Between the Lakes (LBL) National Recreation Area is home to one of America's most sinister Dogman legends. Legend tells of one night during the 1980s when a family was ambushed in their RV. This is what the bite wounds and claw marks had suggested to have occurred. While this sort of evidence does not occur often, locals know that Dogmen have long inhabited the area, with witness accounts tracing back to the early 20th century. The isolation and rural position of the LBL, ringed by dense woods, rolling hills, and curvaceous river fashion lakes, is the perfect environment for a wicked and cunning beast to live.

LBL is not the sole site in Kentucky and Tennessee to have recorded Dogman sightings. Other sites include the Daniel Boone National Forest in Kentucky and the Great Smoky Mountains National Park in Tennessee. These areas have also been terrorized, according to reports of bi-pedal canine forms and unexplained nighttime howls. Campers and hunters in the Daniel Boone National Forest have witnessed bizarre, bi-pedal wolf-like beasts that appear from out of the blackness. In the same manner, travelers in the Great Smoky Mountains have witnessed glowing eyes at night, only to vanish into the trees as fast as they appear.

The terrain of the LBL and the surrounding area provides the perfect environment for the Dogman to go unseen. Thick forests, remote wilderness, and a wide range of wildlife populate the area offering plenty of hiding spots for a beast that shuns human contact. Hunters, campers, and hikers often talk about strange noises echoing through the night glowing eyes peering from the darkness, and quick glimpses of dog-like creatures walking on two legs as they slip in and out of the woods.

These sightings are often explained as a result of wild dogs, whether coyotes or wolves, being present, but most witnesses assume there's something more malevolent at play. It's a terrifying notion to consider that the Dogman is real. An ever-present threat within this part of the globe, and one which has fascinated many of those who travel through the Kentucky and Tennessee woodlands.

OHIO

Nicknamed the Buckeye State, Ohio has a long history of cryptid sightings, and one of the most intriguing is the werewolf or

Dogman-type cryptid. With a lot of forests and rural areas, the state is a wonderful sanctuary for a cryptid to hunt and stalk. And there has been all manner of sightings throughout the years. One of the best-documented reports is that of the Defiance Werewolf in the 1970s, and it is a legendary tale of Ohio's cryptozoology.

The Defiance Werewolf appeared as a two-legged wolf-bodied creature with an intimidating appearance, based on the accounts. The eyewitnesses said that it was roughly 6 feet tall, had a thick pelt of fur and eyes glowing like lanterns that could peer right through the darkness. This monster was said to have been sighted in the rural countryside surrounding Defiance, Ohio, where it was said to have been moving about in the forest and mutilating livestock. Though there are limited official records of this sighting, locals claim the creature was a sign of a catastrophe to come. Since its appearance was generally accompanied by an aura of foreboding, fear and anxiety.

To date, Dogman sightings have been flooding in from various counties in Ohio. In Athens County, several witnesses have come forward who claim to have seen a bi-pedal man-dog hybrid creature. With some of them claiming it was about 6 feet tall and had dark brown hair or fur. In Fairfield County, a group of hikers claimed to have seen an abnormal, bi-pedal canine creature reported having been seen wandering through the woods.

In Franklin County, one resident reported seeing a dogman while driving through the woods in the back of a neighborhood park late at night. While others theorized, maybe it was responsible for a series of seemingly random attacks on animals throughout town. Clinton County has its own Dogman sightings, with some residents stepping forward to say they've seen a large shaggy creature traveling through the forests.

Trumbull County has also been a hotbed of Dogman sightings, with many witnesses describing a creature that is literally a man-dog hybrid. Some have even reported that the creature has been seen walking on two legs, just like a human. Scioto County has also seen several Dogman sightings, with some residents claiming the creature to be around 7 feet tall and with dark, thick fur.

Pickaway County has also been a place where Dogman sightings have been claimed. With several eyewitnesses claiming to have seen a creature that appears to be a dog-man hybrid. Others have speculated that the creature might be the culprit behind a string of mysterious livestock attacks in the region. Dogman has also now made its first appearance in Jefferson County, with reports by residents of a large, hairy animal walking in the forest.

With each fresh case, more people continue to speculate if there is something real about the Dogman, or if it has all been pure fabrication. Some sightings have been dismissed as fake or as mistaken identities by some people, but there may be some reality in those cases as well. What exists are rumors and hype circulating like a wave throughout the state of Ohio. What is real is that all anyone can seem to talk about these days is Dogman.

After all, Ohio's geography is perfect for a creature like the Dogman to make its home. The state's many forests, including the Hocking Hills and the Wayne National Forest, offer a vast and comparatively uninhabited territory for a creature to hunt and roam. Ohio country, comprising rolling hills and twisty roads, offers even better cover in terms of concealment from which a loner-type of being could dwell undetected. Food wise, Ohio offers lots of wildlife with deer, raccoons, and squirrels available that could supply an unlimited quantity of meat as a food source to a Dogman. Its many lakes and streams provide a further source of fish and other aquatic food. It appears that Ohio is a veritable paradise for a bi-pedal creature that runs the woods and the countryside.

MINNESOTA

Minnesota is a land of unlimited trees, lakes and lakes and lakes, and the type of quiet so dense that one may feel oneself all alone there. But surely, no one is ever quite alone out here. Legend from the years has spread into the story, and stories into something so much darker. Legends of the Dogman, a monstrosity on two legs with markings of a wolf. This creature has given fright to many people, foolish enough to roam too deeply into the northern territories.

The scariest accounts are of the Boundary Waters Canoe Area Wilderness and the vast forest along the shores of the Great Lakes. If anything on earth could hide, be unseen, this is where it would do so. The thick canopy pulls the light down into shadows, and the wind runs through the branches like an animal. They talk of ghostly sightings, glinting amber eyes pilfering the moonlight, thunderous growls that shake beneath their feet, and the passing shadow of something too big, too fast, too unnatural.

There is one particular account gleamed from a Dogman Encounters reporting site. It is in an anonymous report from a US Air Force base sometime in early September 1999.

> *"First off, I would like to keep my name confidential; just for the fact that this happened on an Air Force base, and I don't know who reads this stuff. This happened sometime in September of 99. I forgot the exact date. It was early in the month though. It was between 2 and 3 a.m.*
>
> *I was a Security Forces Airman, working 3rd shift, on base patrol. Now mind you, this is an Air National Guard base that I worked at, full-time. It's on the North side of Duluth MN, next to the International Airport. North to northeast is nothing but large wooded areas. Forest areas. The 3rd shift on the base was pretty boring (10 p.m. to 6 a.m.) and us full-timers worked a skeleton crew (usually only 5-6 of us, on 3rd shift). I was in the patrol truck, doing my usual rounds, checking doors and fence lines. Late at night, on the north side of the base was usually*

creepy enough when patrolling by yourself. Anyways, I was on this road, driving towards our baseball field, when my headlights caught a pair of eyes reflecting back at me. They were almost eye level with me, and I was sitting in an F-150. Around this time, a few of the guys had been seeing this huge buck around the property (like a 16 pointer or something around that size). I was about 80 yards or so, when I saw these eyes reflecting back at me. So, I'm thinking it was a big deer. "I gotta see this thing." So, I hit the gas and started speeding towards the field. This is where it all happened so fast. It's almost hard to explain. There was a little slope behind the baseball field. It sloped down, probably about 12-15 feet, into a brush line. The brush went about 30 feet, then turned into a thick tree line. The brush was probably armpit high to me and pretty tough to traverse through, being so thick. As I turned into the baseball field and turned the truck towards the thing, I just caught the rear end of the thing leaping down the slope, below the line of sight of my headlights. The thing was no more than about 20 feet ahead of me when it leaped. All I got a look at was the back end of the thing, and it was big! The best I can do to describe it is to say that it was wolf/dog like in nature. It had a long tail (longer than 2 feet). The hind legs looked exactly like those of a dog; same with the back paws, but the paws were huge. They were bigger than my hands, for sure. The hair/fur was wavy, yet matted and thick. The color was blondish or very light brown. I didn't notice any gray in it, but this all happened within about 2-3 seconds. I sat in my patrol truck for a couple of seconds, confused and thinking, "I know what I saw, but it couldn't have been what I saw." So, I hopped out, with my flashlight, and M-16 rifle, and walked to the edge of the slope. All I heard was the thing running through the woods in front of me, heading in a northwest direction. And this thing sounded like a moose charging through the trees! It made a lot of noise! That's when I started to get really scared; thinking, "If this is some sort of wolf or whatever it could be, my M-16 isn't going to do a thing to this animal." So, I jumped back into my patrol truck as fast as I could and headed back to the S.F. headquarters.

I never told any of the other members about this, for fear of ridicule or being called crazy. There is no way I misidentified this thing! I'm a trained observer, an avid hunter and have worked with animal rehabilitation, with the MN DNR, in the past. I know my animals and the North Woods extremely well. I saw exactly what I saw. And that was the back end of a large wolf/dog thing, that basically had its eyes level with mine, while I was in a patrol truck. The back end was definitely much larger than any of the largest deer or black bears I've seen. The points I remember the clearest were the tail and back paws, as well as the texture and color of the hair/fur. This is my story. I never told anyone for fear of ridicule. I swear it to be the truth!"

Minnesota's boundless wilderness and plentiful food supply give the Dogman all the space he needs to exist. The forests of the state stretch on and on, offering plenty of room for the deer, black bears, and other wildlife. All of which would be available as a food source for a large predator. The rolling, hilly terrain of the northern woods, particularly the Boundary Waters Canoe Area Wilderness, is a perfect cover. Dense underbrush, towering pines, and remote lakes are the environment where something could lie out of sight, moving unseen through the night, beyond the reach of probing eyes.

TEXAS

Texas, with its enormous rural expanses and immense wilderness reserves, has been a breeding ground for cryptid sightings, especially upright walking canines, for decades. The Piney Woods region of the east, with its thick forests and winding rivers, is the ideal place for a creature to wander and hunt. And many sightings of the Dogman have been made there over the decades. From the towering pines to the rolling hills and vast prairies, the Piney Woods region is a varied terrain. But yet it is a relatively unexplored land for this creature to make its home.

Outside of the Piney Woods area, other locations have also been reported. Dogmen have been spotted elsewhere in Texas, including Roscoe, Johnson City, Collin County, Trinity County and Freestone County also have reported sightings.

According to the report on the Dogman Encounters site, this hunter recounts a terrifying experience while coyote hunting at their grandparents' house in Freestone County. While hiking through a neighbor's land, they felt like they were being followed and saw a crouched creature behind trees. As they raised their rifle and looked through the scope, they froze in fear. Panicked, they fired a shot, and the creature stood up and ran away. Later, with their grandfather, they measured the area where the creature stood up and estimated it to be around 7.5 feet tall. This experience has left the author with a lasting fear of night and early morning hours.

Reuben Kimball recounts an encounter with a mysterious creature that occurred on March 20, 2001. While driving home from shopping with his family, he saw a large, brown creature jumping over a barbed wire fence on the side of the road. Initially, he thought it was a deer, but as they got closer, the creature made another impressive jump and continued up an embankment, seemingly looking back at them before disappearing. The author is unsure what the creature was, but it has since been referred to as a "Dogman."

The landscape of Texas is a suitable place for a creature such as the Dogman to live. There are many forests in the state, including the Davy Crockett National Forest and the Sabine National Forest. And these offer a large and untamed area for an animal to roam and hunt. The rolling hills and curving terrain of rural Texas offers a good hiding ground for this elusive creature as well. For food supply, Texas's abundance of wildlife like deer, raccoons, and squirrels offers a plenty of nourishment for a creature like the Dogman. Its many streams and lakes also provide a plethora of fish and other aquatic prey, making Texas hospitable for this creature to run around the countryside and forest.

PENNSYLVANIA

Eyewitness sightings of giant, wolf-like bipedal creatures have been reported in Pennsylvania's Appalachian Mountains. A region famous for its rolling hills, dense woods, and centuries-old history of mysterious creature sightings. The history of Bigfoot sightings in Pennsylvania would seem to show a convergence of cryptid activity and cause some researchers to question whether the two are connected. The Appalachian Mountains cut through enormous chunks of Pennsylvania and create an immense and isolated wilderness region. It contains a great variety of wildlife, such as white-tailed deer, black bears, and coyotes.

There have been several reported sightings of the Dogman in Pennsylvania, and many of these have occurred in the western and central parts of the state. In 2007, hunters in Clinton County claimed to have seen a 7-foot-tall, wolf-like creature standing on two legs with glowing eyes and a foreboding posture. The creature was said to have a heavy coat of fur and a terrifying howl. Although there was no supporting physical evidence from the sighting, it is listed as one of the well-documented Dogman sightings in the state.

Other sightings have been made in Pennsylvania. Sightings were reported in forests in Centre County, where a woman stated that she had encountered a two-legged creature of unusual height that had a wolf's face. The creature was put at about 6 feet in height, with a grayish-brown color, and its eyes glowed in the dark. In another reported case, a Monroe County group of campers reported hearing unexplained howling and spotting a large, wolf-like animal roaming in the woods.

The landscape and the food sources in Pennsylvania are ideal places for a dogman to survive. Pennsylvania's woods have an endless expanse of habitat for deer, black bears, and other animals that would be accessible as food for a large predator-type creature. The isolated countryside of the Appalachian Mountains is also an ideal place for a creature to hide in the rough landscape and dense forests, giving it sufficient cover.

LOUISIANA

The Cajun mythology's legendary "Rougarou" has been likened to Dogman sightings with many cryptozoologists believing they might be related in some way. The Rougarou, however, is a shapeshifter in Cajun mythology, an animal said to inhabit the bayous and swamps of Louisiana out in the rural areas. It was said to be wolf-like, with eyes that glowed like embers, and able to shift from man to beast at will. Even though the Rougarou is largely linked to the rich cultural heritage of Louisiana, certain scientists theorize it can be so much more than legend. That it can indeed be an actual creature witnessed by humans over centuries.

There have been several reported sightings of Dogman in Louisiana, most of which have taken place in rural parts of the state. In 2017, a series of strange events took place on a chicken farm in East Shreveport, Louisiana. Farmers and employees reported encounters with an unknown animal, one they called the "Dogman." The encounters ranged from tracks to dead animals and even shooting at it. Video evidence was reportedly captured during one of the attacks, putting farmers in fear. There have been the same complaints from several other farms in the area. Thus, the increased worry and fear have resulted in greater demands that the police intervene and track the source of the attacks. This was done to provide some sense of security to the farmers, residents, and the rest of the public.

Another reported experience in Louisiana is the Jefferson Parish experience. Where a hunter had a terrifying experience when he was hunting in South Jefferson Parish, Louisiana. Walking along a protection levee system, he heard a growl and saw a pair of eyes with an amber color. The eyes were well above the brush that surrounded it, and upon shining his light, he could see a creature emerging from the woods.

It was bipedal, but its legs were awkward, and it had long arms, with hands that were a combination of bear and man. It had a body covered in black fur with brown undertones, and its ears were pointed with a human type of hairstyle.

When he took a shot from his rifle, the creature stepped back, then gave a blood-curdling scream and started stalking him. He dashed in a run to the street where his truck was parked under floodlights, and the creature lost him. His own granddaddy had gone through something similar when he was 17. And this made him feel he was not entirely by himself, having the strange and inexplicable happen to his granddaddy as well.

The rotting swampy parts of Louisiana offer a handy refuge for some type of unknown creature. The state's vast system of bayous, swamps, and marshes is the perfect place for a monster to lie in wait unseen. Its dense foliage and muddy waters provide more than enough cover. The terrain in Louisiana is characterized by flat plains, rolling hills, and dense forests. This would provide a diverse range of habitats for wildlife, including white-tailed deer, black bears, and alligators. These animals could serve as a food source for a large predator like the Dogman, making it easier for them to survive in the wild.

CANADA

While the United States receives most of the credit for Dogman sightings, the creature has gained increased exposure in Canada, specifically within the provinces of Quebec and Ontario. The vast, open wilderness that cradles these two provinces is a good place for an elusive species to call home. The dense forest, mountainous terrain, and immense amounts of boreal forest in Quebec and Ontario create a harsh environment for human existence. But one that can be exactly the right fit for a mysterious, bi-pedal creature such as the Dogman.

Quebec and Ontario residents have, over the past few years, made reports of enormous, bipedal wolf-like beings spotted along rural roads, forests, and even city fringes. Some of these accounts have been frightening, with witnesses describing scenes where the Dogman appeared to watch them from afar before disappearing into the forest.

As one such report goes, they were driving home from work on a busy road in Hamilton, Ontario, when they noticed a dog crossing the road in front of them. What amazed them was the dog's size, as it was at least 8 feet long from nose to tail, almost the same width as the highway lane itself. They were amazed to see how gigantic it was and could not even imagine a dog growing to such an enormous size. As it vanished into a valley not too far away filled with thick forests, they wondered what breed it was and how it ended up so large. Having looked it up afterwards, they deduced it was a dogman.

Here is another reported sighting taking place in 2020. The group recounts an unusual experience while small game hunting in Alberta. They heard a persistent, repeated coughing sound, similar to a cat hacking up a fur ball, that lasted for quite a while. Then they saw something that they compared to a deformed hyena because of its unusual characteristics. Characteristics that included pointed ears, a cartoonish snout, and ridiculously long fangs. Its eyes appeared amber and abnormal. And its head was something different from the rest of the other animals that they had encountered up to that point. Its hocks resembled a dog, but its front legs were longer than its back legs, and it had its back curved up. They noticed that its front legs, chest, and muscles seemed to be stronger and more protruding than its back legs. The animal's fur was a lighter reddish color. The creature appeared to be circling around them to capture their scent. They have never encountered an animal like this one either before or since, and they are positive that it is not a black bear, which they know. The group never returned to hunt there again due to the strange and spooky feeling. They then discovered a photo on the Internet that looked like the animal they were seeing. A Photo taken near the Wisconsin River, once again validating their belief that they saw something unusual, a dogman.

These sightings are not definitive evidence of the existence of Dogman. They are certainly enough to make a person wonder if an unknown cryptid might lurk deep in Canada's backcountry. Given Canada's vast and uncharted wilderness, it is impossible to rule out the existence of an unknown predator in that landscape. The nation's extensive lands, national parks, and reserves are a home to wildlife such as bears, wolves, and other predators. Maybe there are dogmen living there without the knowledge of man. Further research and investigation need to be conducted to determine the facts behind these sightings and the enigmas of Canada's mysterious wilderness.

CHAPTER 4
PATTERNS IN SIGHTINGS

I never would have taken Dogman as a serious subject. Seriously, I laughed the first time I read about it. A werewolf-like creature spotted all over North America? A campfire monster story at the end of a night, or a fantasy on the part of some cryptid fan. Then I investigated it, interviewing witnesses hearing and reading their testimony. The similarity of the descriptions, the eeriness of the actions, the terror in the voices.

As I progressed deeper into the realm of Dogman sightings, I started observing a strange pattern. The beast appears to be most active during twilight, when the sun rises or sets. The crepuscular boundary times, when the world is illuminated in a golden, warm light, are maybe their best hunting hours.

But twilight hours are not the only time that is notable. Dogman sightings have a definite seasonality too. All creatures possess seasonal activity, but Dogman has a unique cycle. Autumn is especially the season of increased activity for the creature, with Dogman sightings hitting a high from early September until late November. This could be linked to the hunting seasons, which normally take place at this time. Hunters will report sightings in the woods while traveling through familiar forest, only to be confronted with an impenetrable feeling of being observed. Then, the rustling, a low guttural growl, then the realization that they are not alone.

Even more fascinating is the action of the Dogman. It is not an animal acting on instinct, but a calculated and deliberate beast. The manner in which it observes, the manner in which it stalks, as if it knows what it's doing. It's playing a game of cat and mouse with its prey, observing them with this level of unnerving intensity before determining whether or not it will make an appearance. And when it does, it's usually ominous in a way that's both captivating and frightening.

This Dogman, whatever it is, appears to have routines. It's out there in the world in ways we're only just now realizing. And that's what's so disturbing about Dogman. It's not merely a myth and a legend, but something tangible that can inspire fear and wonder in the people who see it. The more I research the world of Dogman sightings, the more questions I'm left with than I have answers. What is this thing, exactly? And what does it ask of us?

Ask ten other individuals what time of day they've seen a dogman, and half of them will say that it was precisely the moment the sun was setting or rising. That slim, golden window of time when the world tilts between light and dark. Some call it the crepuscular witching hour of the wild.

There's something to dusk in the woods. Shadows are impossibly long, stretched across the forest floor like outstretched hands. Every noise, every crack of every branch, every whoosh of wind resonates loudly. The air is thicker, charged with an almost electric energy. It hums deep in some primeval spot, deep down in our bones. We weren't made to be out this late. Perhaps that's why the Dogman terrifies us so.

A Michigan deer hunter once described the night he encountered its gaze. He was packing up, standing on the ground at the base of his tree stand, watching the last of the light leave behind the trees.

The moment that the light had gone, it appeared in front of him. A monstrous creature, dog-headed, but erect somehow. It had breathed out great clouds of steam in the cold air. It did not budge; it did not wink or growl. The creature just glared like it was looking into his very soul.

That's another thing about Dogman, that foreboding stare. They say it watches us, that it is learning us in the dark. It doesn't have to lunge or snarl, but it does just to make sure you know it is there. And it appears to enjoy these liminal moments when night dominates day, or day intrudes into night. That's when it gets nearer to us.

But not only is twilight and dawn the time the Dogman crosses over into our reality. It may be 1 AM, 2:30 AM, or even 3 AM. Or possibly midnight. It's the dead of night when the world is at its weakest. When you are left alone with the darkness. This is when it hides in the shadows, watching and waiting.

Whereas the remote, otherworldly appearances at dusk are brief, ghostly, and unthinkable, nocturnal appearances are fleeting, ominous, and impossible to deny. Some witnesses describe a sensation of being watched while others have reported being paced or pursued.

A Wisconsin truck driver swears in his report he had seen it on an isolated highway at 2:30 in the morning. At first, there was only a form among the trees. And then it quickly dropped to all fours, racing alongside his truck at close to 50 miles an hour. He clutched the wheel, watching in amazement as it matched his pace. And then, in a spooky smoothness, it was on two legs once more, moving only on its hind legs. It flung out a clawed hand, striking against the side of his cab. The truck vibrated from the blow. The driver remained firm. Too scared to brake and refused to even check the rearview mirror.

These early-morning and late-night meetings have a familiar pattern. A pattern of movement, pace, and often some form of aggression. There is a raw, predatory confidence in the Dogman. In the complete darkness of its world, nothing daunts it.

Most animals also have cycles of migrations, mating season, even sometimes a hibernation period. If Dogman is of flesh and blood, then it must have its own cycle, too. Yes, it's plausible for them to have cycles. In Michigan, they say it is a ten-year cycle where sightings are highest, but I found no formidable pattern of that in my research. Due to the distance of the sightings and no verifiable timeline between them, we can deduce that the Dogman does not have a migratory type of pattern.

If fall is when most sightings happen, then fall it is. The air is getting crisp again. Leaves are falling, adding more visibility through the trees. The nights become longer and out comes the Dogman.

Hunters appear to encounter it most during these months. They enter the woods at dawn's early light, their weapons across their backs, waiting for deer or for some other type of game to pursue. Instead, they discover something else, something lurking in the woods, something watching them.

One hunter was walking towards his stand on a chilly November morning when his encounter occurred. He had that sensation, that sensation that tickles at the back of your neck, making your hair rise. That specific sensation of being watched and followed. He stopped to listen, then, before him, something massive moves from behind a tree.

He slowly brought his rifle up to fire at a bear. But when the beast ducked out from around the tree, he recognized it was not a bear due to its height. It was much too tall and was walking around on two legs. One clawed hand clung to the trunk of the tree. A wolf's face, but something more than a wolf. It regarded him and appeared to study him. Then, in an instant, the Dogman turned and vanished. We know Dogman doesn't always attack, but it seems to always let you know it's there.

Winter sightings are rarer, but when they happen, they linger in the witness's mind like frostbite.

A Minnesota farmer woke up one winter morning to an enormous set of tracks in the snow going out to his barn. They were not bear tracks, and they were larger than a wolf's tracks, but still canine. And then, halfway to the barn, they shifted into something now bipedal. He followed them with his flashlight, his heart thudding in his chest, and then nothing. The tracks just disappeared, as if whatever created them had completely vanished from existence.

Winter encounters seem to come with a presence of eeriness, of silence. Typically, no heavy breathing, no snarling, but they still exist. The Dogman passes unseen across the snow, emerging and disappearing almost as if it never happened or was never there at all.

When warm weather occurs, there are fewer encounters, but they do not entirely cease but rather seem to change. This could be due to a birthing season for the creatures. If they are flesh and blood with a steady population, science tells us, they would need to mate. However, I have encountered no reports that included young in the sightings. Perhaps being canine like their offspring are in caves or a large burrow.

Spring and summer sightings are typically near water, like a lake or a stream. Early morning and evening anglers catch glimpses of something enormous on the other side of the water. It appears, it turns around and then disappears silently back into the woods.

A Kentucky man had seen what he thought was a black bear by the river. Then it rose on two legs, much too tall to be any bear. Its eyes fixed on him, blazing with an intelligence that belonged to no beast he had ever met. And then, suddenly, it crouched down on its haunches and vanished into the woods.

The Dogman does not act like any known animal in the wild or one that could be rabid. It does not go for every human it sees. It does not appear to want to kill at random, almost as if it is playing with us.

Most encounters don't end in attacks. They end in terror! It lets you see it and lets you know it could reach you and attack you if it wanted. But then it vanishes, as if that was enough to satisfy its needs.

One woman living in a small town in Ohio woke up to it in her yard. She turned on the floodlights to see if it would jump back. It did not move, but it remained at the forest edge, frozen like death. And then slowly, its mouth twisted into a grin but not a snarl, more like an evil smirk. Then, step by step, the Dogman backed off into the blackness until it was gone.

From much of the witnesses' testimony, even when it tracks you down, it seldom completes the pursuit with an attack. A Michigan teen reported he was pursued across the woods for close to a mile, hearing its lumbering strides behind him, its breath in his neck. But when at last he reached the highway, and the streetlights illuminated him, it just stopped. He looked over his shoulder behind him, but there was nothing there. Only the foreboding darkness of the tree line.

Is the Dogman playing games with us, testing us, or maybe feasting on our fear itself? Or is something worse lurking in the darkness? Perhaps Dogman doesn't need to kill us, even though some still do.

CHAPTER 5
THE MEDIA AND DOGMAN

Something is unsettling about a legend that won't stay buried. Myths that come back year after year and go from person to person. Growing with each retelling like a living, breathing creature. The Dogman is one such legend, a beast of the unexplained that has grown past its origin to a greater thing. A creature shaped and reshaped by the media, the internet, and our desire to believe in something unseen. It is not just a campfire tale, or a forgotten footnote in the history of cryptid folklore. It has become a cultural phenomenon that has captured the popular imagination of people from all walks of life.

As the myth of the Dogman spreads, it becomes self-sustaining and evolving with each iteration to become an expression of our ugliest and forbidden terrors. It's a tale of a monster that defies explanation. A creature that is man and animal, capable of walking on two legs like a man and running as quick and cunning as a wolf. It is called by some to be an omen of doom, a sign of death, and seen by others as a guardian, a protector of the innocent. The truth, however, eludes us, being shrouded in a cloud of rumor and mystery.

But now the Dogman is a contemporary legend, an expression of our desire to be able to believe in something bigger than ourselves and our fascination with the unknown. It's a tale that has been told and re-told, spoken and repeated, until it's embedded in our collective psyche. And yet, in all its ubiquity, the Dogman continues to be a mystery, a puzzle that continues to plague us, to intrigue us still, as we continue seeking the truth.

THE BIRTH OF A MODERN LEGEND

The Dogman was not always a name that appeared on the lips of cryptid enthusiasts, nor on the tongues of folklore enthusiasts. In reality, prior to 1987, there were only quiet whispers in northern Michigan, a distant rumor of a strange story that only a few people had ever heard. It was a legend that was spoken around campfires and in hushed conversations, but never quite reached the ears of a large enough group of people. That was until Steve Cook, a WTCM-FM radio disc jockey in Traverse City, Michigan, took the story to the people.

Cook was not a folklorist or a cryptozoologist, nor was he an experienced storyteller. He was just a guy with a microphone and a notion. He had a flash of imagination that suddenly lifted off when he sat to write and record a song entitled *The Legend* for April Fool's Day of 1987. It was intended as a prank, some local flavor, some combination of real folklore and his own flights of imagination. He had not wanted to make a big impact or whip up a nest of controversy, but something curious occurred. As the song went over the air on the radio, people began phoning in, not to joke or jest, but to verify. Folks started offering their own accounts of the Dogman, claiming that Cook's tune was recounting something which really existed, which they or a person they knew had seen.

The reports flooded in with more being recounted by the day. Individuals claimed they'd seen a large, wolf-like creature on two legs walking along rural roads. Lurking in the darkness of dense woods, even clawing at windows late in the night. The tales varied as much as they were terrifying, and even Cook was taken aback at the response. He hadn't expected the public to react so forcefully. He could never have imagined that his song would resonate on a primeval level, something repulsively true to those who had experienced it. As the years passed and more and more stories came out, *The Legend* became more than a song. It became the beginning of a contemporary ballad, a memorial to the power of a story and the human imagination.

Cook's song resonated with not just the community in the immediate listening area. The song spread both wide and far, like a ripple spreading out on a pond. It reached the lives of many, irrespective of their background or walk of life. It revived an interest in the world of cryptids, and the Dogman suddenly became a name on everyone's lips. The legend surrounding the creature snowballed, fueled by public imagination and the many stories that were told and retold. And at the heart of it all was Steve Cook, the unwitting innocent who had let a monster loose upon the world without realizing what he was doing. He did not wish to leave a lasting legacy, but in doing so, he had discovered something far deeper. An aspect of the human mind that would intrigue and appeal to us for centuries to come.

MOVIES, BOOKS AND DOCUMENTARIES

As with every great monster legend, Dogman became a part of popular culture, permeating the fabric of our shared imagination and winning over the hearts of millions. Never quite achieving mainstream popularity like the Loch Ness Monster or Bigfoot, it clawed its way into film, books, and documentaries. With each putting their own spin on the legend. The status of the Dogman in popular culture is evidence of its longevity as a figure. It's also an indicator that the most fabled of monsters have the ability to both captivate and inspire us.

One realm in which the Dogman still has no permanent impact is that of big cinema. The Dogman remains Hollywood's forgotten stranger, a memory that fades of its vast treasure of folklore and the increasing number of eyewitness testimonies. Werewolves dominate the big screen's canine universe. The Dogman is relegated to the periphery, an afterthought in the master plan of creature features. It is odd, considering the Dogman's unique combination of man and beast, it's human walking and wolf-like running ability in speed and agility, and its foreboding nature.

However, that does not mean the Dogman has had no influence on the film industry. The most well-documented attempts on a film would probably be the 2012 low-budget horror movie *Dogman* from Richard Brauer and its second installment *Dogman 2: The Wrath of the Litter*. While both movies walked the line, they combined the legend with rural horror and tension and an atmospheric sense of horror that lingered long after credits were finished rolling. While they never really hit the mark that other cryptid horror movies achieved, they attest to the enduring popularity of the Dogman. Along with the monster's ability to be the focal point of imaginative reinterpretation.

Lately, the Dogman has spawned a line of low-budget horror movies, which seem to take cues from so called found footage, survival horror, and retro creature features. They simply keep reusing the same formula for these movies: some isolated location, some unlucky people, and the dark figure of something with glowing eyes and blade-like claws. The Dogman tends to be portrayed as an animal-type creature of the dark, an entity that's as frightening as it is imposing. The Dogman itself, however, stays in the background despite its frequent appearances in these films, waiting for someone to give it the credit it so richly merits.

Perhaps the Dogman's lack of a definitive cinematic presentation is the most intriguing feature of its on-screen history. While Bigfoot has more movies under his belt than one can ever hope to count, the Dogman remains waiting for its time in the limelight. It's a monster that needs to be provided with a film that does it some justice. A film that gets beneath its skin and uncovers its mythology in a manner that is authentic and compelling. Until then, the Dogman will continue to be a mystery, a monstrous presence that stimulates and tests our imagination.

The 2000s and 2010s cryptid fever brought an open door of paranormal television shows that flooded viewers and rekindled interest in the world of mysterious creatures. The Dogman, with its creepy mythology and compelling lore, was not immune to this hype. These shows, such as *MonsterQuest*, a highly rated documentary series that uncovered the realm of cryptids, did a story on the Dogman phenomenon. It was done by interviewing witnesses, gathering "evidence," and exploring the dark woods where the monster is believed to live.

These early documentaries offered a combination of fact and fiction, with some trying to be objective and offer plausible explanations for the sightings. Hoaxes, mistaken animals, and mass hysteria were all offered as plausible explanations for the Dogman's existence. Others were more malevolent in their explanations, attributing the Dogman to the supernatural, demon, or something paranormal. These programs used reenactments, ominous music, and scary sound effects to create tension and a foreboding atmosphere, drawing viewers into the realm of the unknown.

Cryptid hunters on YouTube were also important in making the Dogman phenomenon more popular. The fans, equipped with cameras and a thirst for adventure, trekked into the forests searching for proof that the beast existed. Their productions are usually made in a documentary style. They comprise a mix of interviews with witnesses about their sightings and an analysis of any evidence. Some of these videos did not shy away from sensationalizing the events.

Having so many television shows on the paranormal and self-named cryptozoologists on You Tube has actually changed our experience of the Dogman significantly. It's made it a universal interest, so that people all over are sharing and reporting their experiences and ideas on the creature. Dogman, of course, is today a pop cultural reference point, a symbol of the unseen and the unknowable. And for some, the films and documentaries are simply entertainment; for others, though, they are a journey towards examining deeper issues of what may be possible.

Small Town Monsters is a well-known brand in the cryptid documentary genre, popularizing local myths and cryptids. Filmmaker Seth Breedlove founded the firm, which has produced several documentaries about various cryptids and unexplained phenomena. Their goal is to look at these stories with a healthy dose of skepticism and an open mind, trying to report eyewitness accounts and folklore without sensationalism.

Some of their well-known productions include *The Bray Road Beast* (2018), which delves into the sightings of the Beast of Bray Road in Wisconsin. The documentary is based on dramatization, archival footage, and interviews investigating the beginning of the myth and its effect on the local population. The documentary was commended for its ambient storytelling and adhering to documenting various sides of the phenomenon.

Having conducted research on Dogman cryptids, Small Town Monsters produced *The Dogman Triangle: Werewolves in the Lone Star State,* exploring Texas Dogman sightings. The documentary explores the eyewitness testimony and cultural background to the sightings and gives an extended look at the frequency of the legend in the state.

Through their documentaries, Small Town Monsters have contributed to the discussion of the legend of the Dogman. They offer viewers a chance to see these mysterious encounters for themselves through the eyes of those who experienced them. Their work is the best of the independent filmmaker's task of documenting and researching local legend so that such myths continue to be interesting and worth continued inquiry.

THE INTERNET'S ROLE IN DOGMAN STORIES

Prior to the internet, the Dogman phenomenon was a regional one, relegated to the small towns and backwoods where the sightings were claimed to have taken place. It existed in the memories of those who reported having seen it, passed from person to person in small communities. Each tale increased in size as the account changed and grew within the local culture. The myth was forever kept mysterious, descriptions and facts diverging so dramatically from one individual to another. But yet it existed as a cautionary legend shared around the campfires and in whispers. Then, with the emergence of online forums, YouTube, and social media, the Dogman legend was confronted with a tectonic shift. It evolved from a local legend to a global phenomenon that could be shared and interpreted by individuals from all walks of life.

The 2010s proved to be a turning point in developing the Dogman legend. Internet and social media outlets combined to generate the perfect combination of intrigue and terror. The popularity of creepypastas, online horror tales intended to blur the line between reality and fiction, played a large part in this process. These scary stories, often shared on Reddit, paranormal forums, and YouTube, enthralled their audience with their scary stories and creepy atmosphere. Dogman encounters became an extremely popular topic, with individuals worldwide reporting their own personal experiences and stories on the web. The subsequent deluge of user content, such as videos, photos, and written stories, fostered a community, and a shared interest in the legend.

As interest in Dogman sightings increased, YouTube channels focused on cryptid sightings emerged. Channels such as Dark Waters, Mr. Ballen, and Bedtime Stories offered a variety of content, ranging from allegedly authentic eyewitness accounts to dramatized reenactments and even flat-out fabrication. These videos, with the bonus of spooky sketches and foreboding voiceovers, only helped to add to the mystery and intrigue of the Dogman. Whether or not they actually occurred, the impact these happenings had upon the public eye cannot be minimized. The public's imagination and curiosity were only stoked by the sheer volume of media and the often grainy, violent nature of the photographs.

The "encounter videos" which had recently surfaced on the internet were most striking. Blurry, periodic low-light activities. They offered something creeping through the woods late at night, glowing eyes, or anomalous growls on the tape. As it could not be proven that these recordings were valid, they struck a resonating chord in the root fear of the unknown. Were they genuine, I mean who really cared? What was important was the reaction to it, the fear, the intrigue, the excitement of not knowing. When other individuals viewed these videos and sent them to their friends, the social media platform's algorithm noticed. The more users interacted with Dogman content, the more the algorithm promoted it, creating a loop of fascination and terror.

From this, a new generation has been introduced to the Dogman legend. Not in books or on the radio, but in TikTok clips, Facebook chat forums, and Twitter discussions. The legend changed and adapted to suit the shifting tastes and inclinations of the cyber crowd. The Dogman, once a local legend, had now become a global phenomenon, with a presence that appeared to be felt in every nook and cranny of the internet. And as the legend grew and evolved, so the Dogman appeared to be there to stay, a symbol of the dark, shadowy side of man and of fear's resilience.

THE FIRST WRITER

While the internet and social media have been the primary forces behind popularizing the legend of Dogman, books have been a more subtle. A reflective platform to delve into this mysterious creature. Authors, especially those who write about cryptids and folklore, have ventured into the realm of the Dogman with a blend of curiosity and skepticism. They attempt to filter fact from fiction and understand the myth. One of the more prominent voices in early Dogman writing is likely to be that of Linda S. Godfrey. She was an investigative reporter of great diligence who had a deep knowledge of the cultural and historical context behind our conception of the unexplainable.

Godfrey's writing, specifically her book *The Beast of Bray Road: Tailing Wisconsin's Werewolf*, has come a long way in illuminating the Dogman legend. Based on a vast collection of reports of first-hand accounts, interviews, and historical records, Godfrey presented a convincing argument for the reality of an elusive creature. A creature that has been terrorizing Wisconsin's rural landscape for decades. Her book masterfully combines story and critique, interweaving the strands of myth, legend, and first-person narrative into a richly textured tapestry of the Beast of Bray Road. The Wisconsin cryptid with such a close resemblance to the Dogman that many consider them one and the same. In her work, Godfrey throws light not just on the legend of Dogman but also on big questions regarding reality, the power of storytelling, and human nature.

Apart from non-fiction, the Dogman has also appeared in horror fiction books. Authors have used the legend as their inspiration, with some creative liberties turning it into a supernatural being, an ancient curse, or a night monster. In these stories, Dogman typically becomes a monster, eating human flesh and reveling in bringing destruction and chaos to the world. These stories touch us at our darkest phobias, evoking our fear of the unknown and unknowable. Horror authors paint a dark vision of humanity by depicting for us the dark underbelly of Dogman legend, holding us riveted with our worst nightmares and desires. True or not, the Dogman is an engrossing and intriguing topic.

CHAPTER 6
GATHERING EVIDENCE

Gathering evidence is the foundation of any serious attempt to prove the existence of these elusive creatures, called dogman. These enigmatic beings, whether they are Dogman, the legendary Bigfoot, the mysterious Loch Ness Monster, or some lesser-known regional legends like the Chupacabra or the Mothman, remain subjects of debate and speculation due to the lack of indisputable proof. There are thousands of eyewitnesses. They provide colorful and interesting accounts of encounters with the elusive creatures. But we are a world which requires hard, concrete evidence for almost everything. Eyewitness accounts and personal affirmation are not enough to satisfy mainstream science or establish the existence of these elusive beasts. That is where physical evidence, documentation and technology come in. Now the researchers and investigators can go looking for the physical evidence to be confirmed and inspected by the experts.

But we also have to consider beyond the science and technology because there's a very human element to this search. There are many people who spend their entire lives looking for proof, trying to make it through ridicule and skepticism. There are people who have had experiences so profound that they can just not shake them out of their heads.

Every hope, every frustration, every expectation, and every fear are involved. Searching for the unknown is a rush of adrenaline. It's taking a ride on an emotional rollercoaster with frustration around each new setback and fear of what may wait out there in ambush. Even veteran researchers acknowledge they become afraid when they take to dark forests late at night carrying only a flashlight listening for crunching leaves. Each snapping twig might bore something out there waiting.

For the believer, every shred of evidence, however insignificant, is one step closer to vindication. For the skeptic, it's a battle every day to discern fact from fiction. But believers or not, this much is sure: the mystery remains unsolved, and the search must go on.

EXAMINING PHOTOGRAPHIC AND VIDEO EVIDENCE

A picture is worth a thousand words, but when it comes to Dogman research, it also raises a thousand more questions. Is it real? Is it AI? Could it be something else entirely that is misidentified? These are the first thoughts that come to mind when analyzing images and videos of alleged sightings. Our minds struggle to reconcile the often vague or ambiguous visual evidence with the extraordinary claims being made. For years, photographs have been the primary evidence put forth in Dogman and other cryptid investigations. Many of these have become infamous in their own right. Others, like the well-known Patterson-Gimlin Bigfoot footage of 1967, have become legendary. This wobbly film of a big, furry creature walking through the California forest is still generating argument and controversy all these years later. A man in a suit, posing for his photograph to trick the camera? Or a genuine Bigfoot sighting. Only Patterson and Gimlin really know, but such proof is never absolute and has a way of raising more questions than it answers.

Modern technology has made it easier than ever to capture high-quality images. Supposedly allowing even amateur photographers to produce footage that was previously the domain of professionals. However, this increased accessibility to enhanced apps for pictures has also led to a proliferation of hoaxes. It would appear there are those who want to make money from people's interest in Dogman. Photo editing programs and artificial intelligence technology have progressed to the point where near-seamless editing can be done. It's become harder and harder to tell what is real and what is not. As a result, even the experts are left wondering what they are looking at. This only muddies the waters where authentication has become a crucial step in the process of evaluating evidence. To this end, experts now have to analyze a range of factors, including shadows, lighting, and motion, to determine if an image or video is consistent with reality. They also check metadata to verify timestamps and locations and run error-level analysis to detect digital tampering.

But it's not just about proving the authenticity of the picture. Pareidolia sometimes factors in and plays a big role. Then even genuine images can be misinterpreted, as the human mind tries to find patterns, even when they aren't there. A blurry figure in the distance could be a bear standing on its hind legs, or a strange shape in the water might be nothing more than a submerged log. Therefore, it's so important to look at and to consider all the available evidence. With any Dogman sighting, we must be cautious. Photographs and footage, as much as they may be worth, should be accompanied by some form of evidence to support them. They need physical evidence, witness statements, and readings. It is only then that we can begin to assemble a better picture of these unknown creatures and begin to distinguish fact from fiction.

CASTS OF FOOTPRINTS AND OTHER PHYSICAL TRACES

Seeing is one thing, but touching something physical is another. Images are less reliable than physical proof, which is something observable that can be examined and tested. That's why footprint casts have played such a major role in Dogman research. They enable researchers to gather and examine evidence that can give significant information about the existence and conduct of these creatures. A clean print in mud or snow can tell a lot. They can tell us the size of the Dogman, the height from its stride, and sometimes even the weight. Consider Bigfoot, a legend that has captivated individuals on every continent. Plaster molds of gigantic footprints, sometimes with dermal ridges resembling fingerprints, have been gathered for decades. These casts have brought enormous controversy among scientists and skeptics. Some scientists assert these ridges establish the prints were created by a living organism, not carved or stamped imitations. Some others have responded by saying that the hoaxers have only improved at creating tracks that looked real.

But footprints aren't the only physical evidence sought after in Dogman research. Some of the other physical evidence like hair samples, scat, nests, and even reported vocalizations have been collected and analyzed. These sometimes yield fascinating and sometimes surprising results. With some others, DNA analysis has been attempted with intriguing results at times and frustrating results at others. Some of them are from recognized animals such as bears, deer, or opossums, whereas others remain inconclusive. Most fall under the frustrating "unknown primate" or "undetermined species" category. For instance, in 2013, a so-called sample of Yeti hair from Bhutan was analyzed and found to belong to an ancient, but unknown species of bear. Not the monster the public had wished for, maybe, but the find showed new species can still be discovered, even in the field of research into Dogman. It also highlights the importance of rigorous scientific analysis and the potential for unexpected results. None of these should be discredited when they come back "unknown".

Research on Dogman has been on the brink between science and myth for some time. But when there is real biological evidence, it gives credibility to this area of research. When evidence can be physically examined and findings accessed, scientists are then able to distinguish fact from myth and build a better understanding of these creatures. Although the search for physical evidence is sometimes challenging and generally results in inconclusive results, it is an important aspect of Dogman research. Research into this topic continues to break boundaries and expand our understanding of the world.

TECHNOLOGY IN DOGMAN RESEARCH

Drones have revolutionized Dogman searches by providing aerial perspectives that were once impossible to achieve. They allow researchers to survey vast and remote areas with unprecedented ease and efficiency. Dense forests, vast lakes, and rugged mountain ranges can be quickly and thoroughly covered by a drone equipped with high-resolution cameras. Drones provide researchers with an opportunity to search for potential evidence without entering dangerous terrain. It provides a new method of researching Dogman sightings since researchers are now able to patrol areas that were inaccessible or are too time-consuming to reach on foot. In revealing a bird's-eye view, drones are able to assess unusual movement or movement that can be indicators of a dogman.

But drones are not perfect like anything else, and several challenges remain to be overcome in using them in Dogman research. The thick tree cover ensures low visibility, so getting a clear picture of what lies on the ground is not always possible. Moreover, Dogman is reported to be night-time-focused, meaning daytime operations are less successful as the animal will rest or be hiding during this time. Even when a strange occurrence has been caught on camera, the same issues are present, as they are in regular photography. It cannot be easily found out whether the sighting has been genuine or if it has been caused by misidentification or digital manipulation. Like in the case of any mode of evidence gathering, an eye of skepticism must be kept on drone video and several considerations taken prior to making any concrete conclusions.

Despite the problems they can provide, drones have been and continue to be an asset in the search for Dogman. They provide a bird's-eye view of the terrain and the capability to rapidly scan large swaths of land.

Perhaps one of the most thrilling developments in Dogman and other cryptid investigations is thermal imaging. Thermal imaging has transformed the study of these enigmatic creatures. Most reported cryptids, and particularly Dogman-type animals, are said to be warm-blooded mammals, so they will emit heat. Thermal cameras can pick up on heat signatures even in complete darkness, so it is perfect for night work, when the Dogman is said to be most active. This approach has already yielded some curious results, presenting researchers with a new means by which to observe and track prospective Dogman encounters.

In 2000, researchers in the Appalachian Mountains made significant advancements in thermal imaging. They taped footage of an enormous, two-legged beast trooping through trees, its heat pattern revealing it was a living creature. The image was a heat chart with the motion of the beast and thermals discernible but not as definitive images, leaving it unsure who it was. Was it a Dogman, Bigfoot, a bear, or perhaps something completely different? That is the nature of thermal imaging. It reveals motion and heat but not necessarily decisive definition. The tech will be able to sense when there is something around, but sometimes it can't give a simple picture of what that creature looks like.

Despite these limitations, thermal imaging continues to be a valuable asset in research. It allows researchers to detect and track potential Dogman activity in ways that were previously impossible.

Dogman researchers also use sound evidence, as most of these animals are said to make eerie sounds, ranging from loud howls to bizarre yipping sounds. They are described as sounding like nothing else in nature, so researchers are left to wonder if the sounds could be proof of an elusive animal. To record these sounds, researchers place audio recorders in the wilderness, attempting to record something anomalous and shed some new light on the Dogman enigma. Dogman recordings exist to be discovered, but one of the most well-known is of supposed Bigfoot calls. They are called the Sierra Sounds, a collection of sounds recorded back in the 1970s in California's Sierra Nevada Mountains.

The Sierra Sounds tapes contain strange chatter and grunting noises that some believe to be actual Bigfoot communication. In my opinion, it sounds almost like Samurais talking to each other. The tapes have been analyzed by linguists and audio experts, who've determined that they sound nothing like any other known animal call. Some experts have said they have the structure for being some type of language. The noises are not like anything ever heard in the wild before, and some think they could be proof of an unknown species. But skeptics say that it is also conceivable that pranksters created the sounds, using methods like sound manipulation and vocal manipulation to produce a convincing hoax. This points out the difficulty of interpreting sound evidence, as it is easy to mix up fake recordings with real ones. But we must remember, these came from the 1970s.

Improvements in the methods of analyzing sound have greatly contributed to making it possible for researchers to segregate the recordings into individual frequencies. This enables them to easily compare them with any known species. If the sound falls outside the range of any known animal, then it will further strengthen the argument of something new. That is a great help in hunting for proof of the Dogman. It enables scientists to recognize patterns and anomalies that can suggest an as-yet unknown species. Again, however, as with all evidence, it is the interpretation that counts. Scientists need to be ultra-cautious in considering the context and situation of the recording, and indeed the possibility of human error or tampering.

By combining thermal imaging and audio recordings with other forms of evidence, such as eyewitness accounts and physical signs, researchers can build a more comprehensive picture of these creatures and their habits.

As technology continues to develop, drones, thermal imaging and audio recording analysis will play an increasingly important role in the research into Dogman. New technologies will provide new information and new areas of investigation that were previously unachievable.

CHAPTER 7
DNA TESTING & TYPES

I've spent years thinking about the strange, the unexplained, and the things that creep just outside the edges of what we call reality. Some of us chase shadows. Others chase monsters. Me? I'm drawn to what lies in between. Things like the Dogman. And few beasts conjure up as much horror, fear, and awe as the Dogman does. Eyewitness accounts tell of an enormous, wolf-like creature with glowing eyes, a nearly supernatural presence, and the ability to disappear like mist. Most claim it moves on two legs, but a few offer descriptions of a quadruped not bipedal.

But the common theme is that it significantly resembles a wolf, and not in some detail that can be easily explained. Dogman's ability to blend into its surroundings and camouflage itself has raised many questions regarding its type of being. But what if it exists beyond the legends? What if it exists, and there are some truths to these tales?

That's where DNA testing must enter the picture. Unlike grainy photos or shaky phone videos, DNA doesn't lie. It doesn't care what we believe. It just tells you the truth, if we let it. DNA results don't lie. If we could get our hands on just one good sample of blood, hair, saliva, or scat we might finally crack this mystery wide open. DNA could tell us if this thing is part wolf, part human, something entirely new, or something we've seen before but misunderstood. But that is one gigantic "if." Gathering valid evidence, storing it, and making sure it is contamination-free is a task which requires meticulous planning and know-how.

Searching for evidence is more than just a weekend hike through the woods. It's methodical, slow, and usually unrewarding. But every scratch on a tree, every strange print in the mud, every unsettling howl in the night, that's where you look. When you find something, whether it's a tuft of hair or a smear on a branch, the next step is protecting it. That means sterile gloves, clean tweezers, sealed containers, and ideally, a DNA field collection kit. Even a single stray human hair or a dog's fur can ruin a sample. Contamination is the enemy. You only get one shot at making this count.

Let's discuss the best methods to gain potential Dogman DNA samples before we discuss actual-world Dogman and cryptid DNA testing. Without an adequate sample, even the greatest lab in the world won't do us any good. In order to get a good sample, we have to consider where the Dogman is reported to live. This can include hiking deep into heavy forests, walking across rocky terrain, or even into extremely limited access areas. We must keep a sharp eye out for anything. The Dogman's reported ability to disappear into thin air would show that it is most likely a very deceptive and cunning beast.

The process of gathering samples requires some special tools and methods to lower the chances of any possible contamination. This could involve using items like clean swabs, gloves, and containers to collect your samples. You should consider purchasing a DNA field testing kit, as this is the easiest way to get and control your samples. You'll also need a well-planned approach when searching for proof. You need to consider where the Dogman lives. This might include setting up some hidden cameras, listening to recorded sounds or even carrying out planned searches in areas where people claim to have spotted the Dogman.

At the end of it all, the only way to truly tap into Dogman's secrets is based on the procurement and analysis of good quality DNA samples. Then maybe half the battle will be won. Yet, even with the assumption that we succeed at getting a quality DNA sample, there is still a need to scrutinize the various challenges surrounding the DNA testing itself. That takes the form of utilizing expensive specialized equipment, human resources, and materials for conducting the tests. It's a daunting challenge, but one which might ultimately lead to a tremendous leap in our understanding of this elusive creature.

To prove the Dogman exists, we don't need a body, we only need a piece of it, something physical. That means finding and preserving some type of biological material, including hair, saliva, blood, or scat. Each of these comes with its own advantages and challenges to get.

Hair can be the easiest evidence in the search for Dogman. If this creature is real, it sheds, just like any other living being. That's a basic part of nature, and it gives us a potential glimpse into its existence. You might find hair samples almost anywhere. Think about where the Dogman scratched a tree, rested, or got into a scuffle with another animal. For instance, if we happen to find a tree whose trunk has been scratched, if we take a closer examination of the surrounding area, we might be able to find a hair sample that could belong to the Dogman. If we obtain strange prints, we may look around them and obtain a hair sample that would offer a critical clue.

But there is a big issue with only using isolated hair samples. Hair without the root (root of the hair) does not contain nuclear DNA, the genetic material that gives us a definite identification of the species it belongs to. Without the root, we have only mitochondrial DNA (mtDNA), which only gives us a partial genetic snapshot. This can complicate the identification of the species and even cause misidentification. For example, mitochondrial DNA could be identical between species so that it would be impossible to identify the exact species from which the hair was drawn. It could come back as a primate, but which primate would be unknown.

Both mitochondrial and nuclear DNA have vital roles to play in bridging the gaps of Dogman's genetic makeup. Nuclear DNA, found in the cell headquarters, contains most of the organism's genes and plays a vital role in understanding complicated traits and diseases. Unlike mtDNA, which is inherited from mother to child and follows maternal family lines. Since it makes a copy quicker, mtDNA is of particular importance in retracing the history of evolution of life and family lines between groups and species.

Contamination is also a major problem. One strand of human or dog hair, or even a single spot of dust, can ruin your sample. These samples would be useless for any DNA testing. Gloves, sterilized tweezers, and sealed storage bags are needed when handling potential evidence due to this. Minimizing the chance of contamination is required to maintain the integrity of the sample. If we recover a potential Dogman hair sample, it should be sent immediately to a DNA lab, so it doesn't break down. The sooner we can test the sample, the better chance we have of recovering usable genetic information and tracing its source.

To get the best chance of recovering a viable hair sample, you need to be methodical in your search. This may mean searching your surroundings, looking for any sign of Dogman's existence, like scratch marks on trees or strange smells. We also need to watch our own presence and do everything we can to keep our impact on the environment as minimal as possible. The human presence tends to taint potential evidence unwittingly. By being meticulous in our hunt and the treatment of any potential evidence, we can improve the likelihood of having a hair sample that yields informative information regarding the Dogman.

If you can get some saliva, you just won the DNA lottery. Saliva offers a potentially rich source of genetic material in the search for the Dogman. If this creature were to bite into something, such as a carcass, a tree, or even a discarded can, it could leave behind a DNA-rich trail of spit. Since gathering saliva requires tedious and meticulous work, this is where patience comes into play in the investigative work. Saliva would be collected using swabs that are designed for forensic sampling. These swabs would be made of a sterile, non-abrasive substance that will not cause any damage to the DNA when being collected.

The key to successful saliva collection is gentle collection. Don't rub too hard, or you risk damaging the DNA. This requires a delicate touch and a thorough understanding of the collection process. After collecting, the sample must be dried and placed in a sterile container before heading to the lab. This is a critical step, as any contamination or degradation of the sample could render it useless for DNA analysis. The container must be airtight, and the sample must be stored in a cool, dry place to prevent bacterial growth and degradation.

However, like most everything else, there's a catch as saliva degrades fast. Heat, moisture, and bacteria will break it down, so time is your enemy when it comes to collecting saliva samples. A good sample needs to get frozen or processed quickly, ideally within a few hours of collection. This requires a well-planned and coordinated effort, with a clear understanding of the collection process and the importance of timely sample handling. If we're lucky enough to collect a saliva sample, we must act quickly to preserve it for DNA analysis.

When it eats, it poops and scat, or animal droppings, may be a smelly subject, but it's well worth it in hunting for the Dogman. Scat is a goldmine of DNA, with digestive tract cells that can yield nuclear and mitochondrial DNA. It has all kinds of information about the animal's genetics, what it consumes, what it comes into contact with, and its health. For example, certain plant material or insect fragments in the scat can inform us about what the animal eats. And certain parasites or bacteria can inform us about their environmental exposure.

But collecting scat is not for the faint of heart. There is a certain comfort level required when working with and examining feces. You also need to have an understanding of the collection and storage procedures. Scat must be stored in sterile tubes, refrigerated, and examined quickly to prevent degradation and contamination. The biggest problem, however, is distinguishing Dogman scat from known animals. Dogman scat may be mistaken for bear scat, wolf scat, or big dog scat, which would render any subsequent DNA analysis worthless.

To be able to solve this problem, it requires seasoned researchers and analysts who understand the nature of different animal scats. This could include the study of texture, color, and consistency of the scat, its composition and structure. Dogman scat, for instance, can be differentiated from wolf scat through size, shape that is elongated, or the inclusion of certain plant material. By highlighting the general characteristics of the scat of various animals, scientists will enhance the likelihood of correct identification and analysis of the samples.

When it comes to any DNA testing, blood is the proverbial smoking gun. If you're fortunate enough to find Dogman blood, you're in business. Blood carries full nuclear DNA, which is more than enough to definitively prove the existence of a new species. But blood is a hard thing to get, because it's not usual. Blood may be located where documented Dogman sightings took place, particularly if there was an injury involved. It could be a gunshot wound from a hunter, a mishap from hitting an animal on the road, or a battle with another predator. If that is the case, there could be blood, but one must be careful and take precautions in getting it.

Just like all other types of DNA samples, proper collection is vital when it comes to blood samples. A clean, dry cotton swab, a sterile vial, and quick refrigeration are non-negotiable. If you're not prepared, you risk contaminating the sample, which could lead to inaccurate results or even render the sample completely unusable.

If blood soaks into something, such as dirt or fabric, you must take a different approach. In this situation, you may need to cut or scrape the material to collect a sample. This requires a high degree of care, as you need to avoid contaminating the sample while also ensuring that you collect a good representative sample. Once you've collected the sample, it's essential to store it properly. This might involve placing the sample in a sterile vial, sealing it, and refrigerating it immediately. Bacteria can degrade the sample quickly, so it's essential to act fast to preserve the integrity of the possible Dogman blood sample.

Dogman DNA research is not being done in isolation but is instead standing on the shoulders of earlier cryptid research. A great example of this is the Sasquatch Genome Project, which had the purpose of gathering DNA samples at supposed Bigfoot locations and examining them. Although some questioned the success of the project, it did open doors for further research on the genetic composition of cryptids. By examining what happened with the Sasquatch Genome Project and what they achieved through it, researchers can gain a great deal of insight into what did and didn't work. They can take this information and use it in their own research on the Dogman.

The Sasquatch Genome Project was led by Dr. Melba Ketchum and was one of the most ambitious cryptid DNA studies ever attempted. The project claimed to analyze over 100 alleged Bigfoot DNA samples, and the results were nothing short of groundbreaking. According to Dr. Ketchum and her team, the study revealed a hybrid species of half-human and half-unknown primate. However, the project's findings were met with intense scrutiny, and the study faced many challenges that ultimately raised questions about its validity.

Among the biggest issues with the project was its rejection through peer review. Despite having some very high ambitions, the study was rejected by some of the world's top scientific journals due to the methodology and interpretation of the results. Claims of contamination and misinterpretation of data also tainted the project. Critics charged the project with using well-known animal DNA, such as human, opossum, and bear, in an improper manner to be considered as new. Those were among some of the accusations made against the validity and credibility of the study.

However, even with the controversy surrounding the project, there are some scientists who feel that the approach was sound, but the implementation was poor. They feel that the findings of the study, though intriguing, were not sufficiently backed up by the data. Using so-called Bigfoot DNA samples by the project, which were sometimes gathered by amateur scientists or enthusiasts at times, also left questions about the quality and purity of the samples. In addition, the analysis of the DNA sample used in the research was done with a comparatively small sample size that might not have captured the larger population of potential Bigfoot.

The single most important lesson to be learned from the Sasquatch Genome Project is that DNA analysis is only as good as the collection, storage, and analysis of it. If we're going to work with Dogman DNA, we need to do it right. That is, if there is rigid sampling and analytical protocol, being able to gather good-quality DNA samples, handling and storing samples properly. That also involves honesty and transparency on methodology and outcomes and being willing to respond to challenges and questioning by the science community.

Last but not least, the Sasquatch Genome Project is a cautionary tale about the inflexibility and imprecision of science. Although project findings were intriguing, ultimately, they became dismissed as a result of methodology failure and peer review absence. From project errors, we should build a good and reliable practice of DNA sampling that will provide us with a better chance at truth regarding the existence of the Dogman.

In another cryptid example, Bryan Sykes, a respected geneticist from Oxford University, ran a project testing supposed Yeti samples. Hair collected from high in the Himalayas tested out as belonging to a species of bear that might be a hybrid of polar and brown bears. Though not proof of a Yeti, it showed how something misidentified could still lead to scientific surprises. This is how unpredictable the hunt can be. You go looking for monsters and sometimes find undiscovered hybrids, or even nothing at all. But the work matters.

When we look at what DNA studies outside of cryptid research, we can see there are great advances being made in the study of man which can entirely change how we view cryptids like the Dogman. Homo sapiens migrated out of Africa roughly 50,000 years ago, but scientists have now discovered that some chose to remain thus revealing a previously unknown lineage that stayed isolated for millennia. Genetic researchers are now analyzing skeletons recovered from the Takarkori rock shelter in present-day Libya to learn more about this ancient, secluded population.

Nada Salem, a PhD student with the Max Planck Institute for Evolutionary Anthropology, led the study, shedding light on a new chapter of the human story. Ancient DNA reveals a group that survived in northern Africa for tens of thousands of years in isolation, previously unknown to science. While other Homo sapiens leaving Africa were intermingling with human populations and related species across the globe, this group remained genetically distinct.

So where are we? What does this say about the possibility of a bipedal canine? We know what we have to do, and we know how to do it, but do we have a plan of action? In order to make Dogman DNA testing work, we must approach the problem with a general plan that encompasses a number of things.

Things such as systematic fieldwork by trained individuals in teams. They can then be deployed into hot-spot areas to gather potential evidence, using a scientific and systematic strategy to ensure every sample is gathered and processed appropriately.

It needs proper storage and a chain of custody. Each sample should be handled as if it were a crime scene investigation. That includes using specialized equipment and storage facilities for maintaining the integrity of the samples.

Any subsequent DNA attempts will require independent laboratory verification from several labs. This is required to authenticate the findings of any DNA test to provide credibility and accuracy. This includes utilization of various methods of testing and comparison of results to eliminate any mistakes or inaccuracies.

The findings should be accepted by mainstream science journals to be published so that the findings are exposed to open scientific criticism. Science should not have shortcuts and secrets. All findings should undergo intense peer review with open and transparent communication between scientists, laboratories, and the scientific community.

If Dogman exists, DNA analysis will confirm it. If it doesn't, DNA analysis will confirm that too. Regardless of which path, the pursuit of scientific fact is the only way to find out the truth about this mysterious creature. As we set out, I hope the truth is out there, waiting to be found. And I'm not the only one. I'm sure all of you will join me in hoping for this. But faith is not fact. That's why DNA testing is necessary. It's our best hope of uncovering the truth behind Dogman.

CHAPTER 8
ZOOLOGICAL AND ANTHROPOLOGICAL PERSPECTIVES OF DOGMAN

Hundreds of years have gone by since humans started to report sightings of a bipedal wolf-like creature known as Dogman. These reports have caused heated controversy and intrigue. One school of thought is it is a paranormal being. A creature that defies explanation and pushes the boundaries of our understanding of the natural world. Another belief is that it is an as-yet-undiscovered species that has somehow evaded scientists and wildlife experts. But the skeptics hold the opinion that it's simply a misidentification of an already known creature. While another group believes it to be a giant hoax committed by hundreds, maybe even thousands, of eyewitnesses.

But when we look at Dogman sightings compared to what we know of wolves, bears, and dog-wolf hybrids, we find patterns which raise further questions. The accounts of Dogman vary, but most of them share a common factor. It is wolf-like, bipedal, and is approximately 5 to 7 feet tall. Other reports even state that it has a muscular physique, with a thick coat of fur which is frequently black, brown, or gray. Others report it has a more human face with nearly human-like eyes.

The sheer number of sightings that have been reported when combined with the descriptions hints to us there could be more to the Dogman legend than what appears at first glance. Is it a relic species, a leftover from an earlier time that has somehow managed to exist in secret? Or is it a genetic mutation, an animal that is born with characteristics unlike anything found in the natural world? Or just us humans simply unfolding our fantasies, using the archetypes of ancient culture and our universal fear of the unknown? The further we dig into Dogman mystery, the further we are pushed to the edge of our scientific understanding.

DOGMAN VS. KNOWN ANIMALS

We know from the eyewitness accounts Dogman it is said to be a tall, muscular creature covered in fur. One that walks upright like a man but with the head of a wolf. Its eyes are often described as glowing, which may suggest it has heightened nocturnal vision. Clawed human-like front hands with pointed ears, and a foreboding presence complete the image.

Compared to these characteristics, the nearest thing it would be like is some kind of canine. This most likely would be a wolf (Canis lupus). These are fierce, intelligent predators that are known to be resilient and versatile in many climates. Even though they have many powerful physical and cognitive traits, they do not walk on two legs for long periods of time. They can stand on two legs temporarily. But this is typically to play or as a signal of aggression, showing their highly developed flexibility and coordination. This is usually observed in wolf packs, especially in superior and inferior animal relationships. Standing, if only briefly, showcases the wolves' very developed physical ability as well as their capability at intricate social interaction.

Wolves have a common ancestry with domesticated dogs, coyotes, and even foxes, all of whom are part of a larger canid family. This is stated in their physical features, behavior, and genetics. But the concept of Dogman as a product of the wolf lineage is quite fascinating. If that were the case, it would need substantial anatomical modifications to support bipedalism. It would demand a more upright spinal orientation, wider pelvis, and stronger legs in order to hold the upright position and stay balanced. All of this would be massive and would demand thousands or millions of years of evolution. There isn't such a canid documented to express such a transformation. So, it seems that a naturally evolved upright walking wolf isn't probable unless it is some unknown-to-us species with its own unique evolutionary history.

The idea of an unknown species with its own unique evolutionary chain may not be so far-fetched. New species are being formed and reclassified all the time in the science of biology. The Amazonian rainforest alone contains an estimated 10% of the planet's plant and animal species, a large majority of which are yet to be classified. Likewise, the Himalayas are said to have a substantial number of undescribed species. There is a possibility of an invisible species of canids with an exceptional evolutionary history like Dogman.

MISIDENTIFICATIONS & HYBRIDS

When we begin to look at misidentifications, we must also look at bears (Ursidae) due to their muzzled faces. Bears do often stand on two legs, particularly grizzlies and black bears, as a means of intimidation or to gain a higher up food source. They can appear extremely tall when on two legs while appearing foreboding in low lighting conditions. This might be one of the Dogman's favorite myths to be played off as a bear. It is not surprising that frightened witnesses may misidentify an irate bear as something else, especially if it occurs during poor lighting conditions. Although a bear's snout differs from a dog's, the trauma and adrenaline can distort one's vision.

The situation that a bear might be confused with Dogman becomes more plausible when we consider areas where a large bear species exists. Where grizzlies or black bears are around, it is not unlikely that witnesses might have seen one of these enormous animals. Then, out of fear, they incorrectly identified it as a dogman. However, there are a few glaring flaws in this theory. Bears have a more rounded head with shorter noses, and an entirely different limb formation than Dogman. They have differently placed ears, and they do not have the distinctive "mane" or ruffly fur pattern so frequently reported. The Dogman is said to have a more human-like gait and proportionate limbs. This discrepancy questions whether it would be possible for a bear to be mistaken for a dogman. And more specifically, in instances where the animal was observed running quickly on two legs.

The notion that a bear could run fast on two legs at high speeds is highly improbable. Bears of any type would be restricted by their physical structure and their body composition. Even though bears are capable of running at high speeds, they would have to be quadrupedal running on all fours. They are not well-suited for running long distances or can they walk bipedal for long distances. The Dogman legend generally presents the creature as being capable of quick and easy movement, running on two legs at the speed and stealth of a dog. These distinctions show us the challenge of explaining the Dogman sightings as sightings of a familiar animal, a bear. Again, this implies that perhaps there is more to the legend than was previously believed.

We are certain that wolf-dog hybrids exist, but they are not bipedal. This only goes to confirm the idea that the legend of Dogman is perhaps founded on an animal outside the realm of regular biology. But still, let us suppose a genetic disorder, something like a rare mutation or a magical bloodline that can account for what has been observed as a Dogman. Hybridization of radically differing species is not unusual, and the following number of examples shows the viability of crossbreeding between various species.

The grolar bear, for example, is a cross between a polar bear and a grizzly bear that yields a mix of traits from the parent species. The liger is also a cross between a lion and a tiger that yields features from both species, including its size, coat pattern, and temperament. These instances show that hybridization of dissimilar species is possible under certain circumstances. Visualize if you can, a time in the evolutionary chain where a dire wolf and some type of primate are bred. This cross may have then given rise to an animal possessing the traits of both.

Dogman just might be a genetic throwback, or hybrid that cannot be categorized in any normal way. A creature with a primate-like posture, but canine in appearance. This would be amazing, but perhaps a little too much for nature to accomplish? Actually, there are several non-primate animals that have developed to display traits which are primate-like. Animals such as the aye-aye, a lemur species whose middle finger is long and bony and used to catch insects. Likewise, there are certain canid species, such as the Southeast Asia dhole, that have been seen standing on their hind legs to move upright, then walk on their hind legs. These are not necessarily something we'd ever really consider as a Dogman, if you know what I mean. But they do illustrate that there's a range of possibilities if you're thinking about how primate-like features and bipedalism might arise in canids.

The potential of a genetic flaw or hybrid anomaly which cannot be classified is plausible. But then it poses some very pertinent questions about the nature of evolution and the diversity of life on earth. By considering the potential of a creature such as Dogman, it forces us to ask questions about what we know of the various species, hybridization and genetic crossbreeding. Although the idea of a creature like Dogman sounds like science fiction, it also tells us that nature is full of surprises. And that there is still so much to discover and learn.

A RELIC SPECIES

What if Dogman is a relic species or a relic hybrid species? After all, we are still finding evidence of species long to have thought to be extinct. Evolution is a dynamic and constantly unfolding process, leaving remnants of species long thought extinct. The coelacanth is a fish thought to have gone extinct 66 million years ago with the dinosaurs. But it was discovered alive in 1938, off the coast of South Africa. This astonishing find shook the scientific world, questioning our knowledge of the evolutionary past and destiny of all the species thought to be extinct.

The coelacanth, or "living fossil," is a remarkable specimen of a biological species that has survived and thrived undetected in the world today. Mainstream science thought it to be extinct for millions of years. Its prehistoric fish's body hardly changed since dinosaur times, with its lobe-finned form and scaly coat. Its discovery has also given us fantastic insight into the evolutionary history of life on our planet. Which raised significant questions regarding the nature of extinction and the resilience of a species.

The discovery of the coelacanth has many implications for our understanding of the Dogman legend. If a species that has been extinct for millions of years can still be discovered alive, it's not out of the question that a creature like Dogman might be a relic of an ancient species as well. Currently, there is no direct fossil evidence pointing towards an upright-walking canine, but that doesn't exclude the possibility. Fossil records are incomplete, and scientists still piece together the life history of the Earth. A giant ape that became extinct, Gigantopithecus, is commonly speculated to have evolved into Bigfoot, for instance. Might some other unknown type of canine have co-evolved with early humans or Bigfoot and adapted to blend in and thrive behind the scenes?

Another possible evolutional scenario is the Amphicyonidae, also known as bear dogs. These massive, powerful predators roamed the Earth millions of years ago, during the Miocene Epoch. They are assumed to have been quadrupedal due to their skeletal structure. But with such a sturdy body and powerful legs, we can't rule out the possibility of an evolutionary divergence. One that could have led to bipedalism in a surviving offshoot. Amphicyonidae were not directly related to modern canines, but their fossil record suggests that they were a distinct group of predators.

If the Dogman is a relic species, it would have needed to remain hidden. This may be a little more difficult of a task in the modern world, but not in the relative past. However, it's not impossible that a species could have adapted to a more solitary lifestyle, avoiding human contact and living in remote areas. The idea of a hidden species is not new. There are many examples of animals that have managed to survive and thrive in the wild, despite being thought to be extinct or rare, like the Silver Back Gorilla.

The concept of such a mysterious creature as the Dogman reminds us of how evolution operates and how animals adapt in order to survive in their environment. If the Dogman exists, then it would not be surprising if it evolved with time so that it could survive. It would not be surprising either if this evolution continued. It becomes feasible for us to visualize a scenario in which a creature such as Dogman might have evolved as a relic of the past. Yet it remains mostly out of sight but still present in the modern world.

CHAPTER 9
THE BIOLOGICAL HYPOTHESIS

The Dogman treads the fine line between fact and myth, frequently positioning itself in that space where science and myth converge. There are some animals once regarded as a cryptid, such as the giant squid, who were initially debunked as sailor's tales. But were later found to be actual, their enormous bodies and tentacles proven by scientific exploration. Others, like Bigfoot or the Dogman, are mysterious and most individuals wonder whether they even exist. If the Dogman exists, it poses a very basic, but yet powerful question: What is it? More precisely, might it actually be an unknown species, the forgotten relic who has been hiding in plain sight for centuries?

We know from the reports most witnesses describe the Dogman as a large, wolf-like creature with distinct canine features. Features that include a wolf-like head, sharp teeth, and piercing eyes. However, there is one major difference which sets it apart from other known canids. It walks on two legs. This is where biology resists strongly, since bipedality is a very unusual characteristic outside of primates. Did evolution create a bipedal canine, one that evolved into an upright walker such as us humans? If so, what would be its behavior, diet, and role in the ecosystem? Would it be a scavenger, roaming about devouring carrion and small creatures, or a predator, stalking its food like a wolf? Or maybe it would be an odd omnivore, consuming a combination of plants and animals.

In order to get an even better glimpse into this, let's speculate on the hypothetical biological composition of the Dogman. If, in fact, it is indeed a bipedal canine, it must have undergone some sort of modification that would enable it to support itself on its hind legs. These may also include a more vertical body posture, more muscular back and legs, and a restructuring of its skeletal framework to adapt to its new mode of locomotion. It can also have some other specific traits, such as an even more flexible spine, arms and hands. And maybe an adapted stomach that allows it to consume a large variety of foods.

WHY IS A BIPEDAL UNUSUAL?

As we look at the potential for the Dogman, we are compelled to look at the confines of what we know about biology and evolution. If a biped canine is actually a reality, it would blow apart our existing knowledge of the evolution of bipedalism and the evolution of human anatomy. But do we really know all there is to know about this process?

Walking on two legs isn't just about standing up. It's a structural overhaul that requires a fundamental transformation of the body's skeletal, muscular, and nervous systems. Evolution will typically favor efficiency, and running on four legs is simply more efficient for running fast, running far, and maintaining stability. Wolves, bred to run, pursue prey, and run down quarry, use four legs to impart maximum power and quickness. They are adapted for explosive bursts of acceleration, tight turns, and prolonged running at high speeds, so four-legged running is best suited to their lifestyle.

We know that being a bipedal creature is actually a rarity on this planet when compared to the rest of the known species.

Kangaroos and some rodents, like jerboas (small desert mouse), have developed a unique hopping gait that allows them to cover great distances with ease. But they don't have a steady walking gait like humans do. Bears and raccoons can stand or take a few steps upright, but they aren't built for long-term bipedal movement. Their bodies are adapted for climbing, digging, and manipulating food, rather than walking on two legs for extended periods.

For the Dogman, anatomical changes not found in any other type of canid would be necessary. These would involve a changed pelvis, which would have to be more vertical to bear the body weight and allow for effective upright walking. This would involve radical changes in the shape and structure of the pelvis, including the ilium, ischium, and pubis bones, which form the hip bone. A canine that has become bipedal would require altered leg muscles, a different type of muscle group, and point of attachment for movement and balance. Leg muscles would be reorganized for the altered gait, stronger back and leg muscles for standing erect.

Now we must consider the feet, since a bipedal dogman's foot anatomy would also be different. It would not have the same combinations of the digitigrade (toe-walking) and plantigrade (heel-walking) forms of locomotion which are found in other animals. A bipedal canine must have its entire foot to support its body weight. It must also be able to flex its toes in some way to facilitate balance and movement. This would require a dramatic alteration in the foot's anatomy, such as the bones, muscles, and ligaments.

This would mean it either evolved into bipedalism independently or it represents an entirely new offshoot of canid evolution. This would have significant implications for our understanding of the evolution of bipedalism. It would also raise questions about the ecological role of the Dogman and how it interacts with its environment. This would also open the door for potential other, as-yet-undiscovered species to exist in similar environments.

POTENTIAL HABITATS & SOCIAL BEHAVIOR

Let's say the Dogman has evolved into an upright bipedal creature. What type of habitat does it prefer? Is it crepuscular, nocturnal, or maybe a little of both? Most eyewitness reports of the Dogman place it in forests, moving through the trees at night, which may suggest nocturnal behavior. It is consistent with the predator's concealment, in which the hunter conceals itself by using darkness to hunt and pursue its victim.

Wild canids and wolves like to roam during the crepuscular hours of dawn or dusk. But a bipedal predator like the Dogman may require a cover of darkness in which to conceal themselves. This would only be more applicable if it is self-aware enough to understand what humans are capable of doing. Lurking under the cover of darkness would allow the Dogman to remain mostly undetected.

A solitary or a small family lifestyle would also make sense for the Dogman. Wolves rely on pack hunting because they chase down prey over long distances. However, if the Dogman is likely a stalking predator, it wouldn't need cooperation. Instead, it would use its wit and quickness to ambush its prey, such as the lone predator like the leopard or polar bear. These predators employ the skill of surprise and stealth to attack their prey, and the Dogman could do the exact same. With the amazing speed that it is said to possess and using trees and natural cover to establish ambushes, the Dogman could be a very effective hunter.

Another option is the Dogman is not entirely a meat eater but rather an omnivorous opportunist, eating small critters, carrion, and vegetation. Wolves are generally endurance hunters, wearing down their quarry over long distances, but being bipedal could change that tactic. Given its speed, it probably wouldn't have to chase over long distances. It might instead use its standing position to survey its ground, looking out in the distance for its potential prey or source of food. With its intelligence and adaptability, the Dogman might be an excellent hunter.

As with most alpha predators, the Dogman's actions may be dictated by its establishment of a territory. Wolves, coyotes, and foxes all establish territories, and a large, reclusive predator like the Dogman would have to possess a secure zone, perhaps miles in diameter, to prevent competition. This would be an excellent explanation as to why the sightings are so infrequent. If the Dogman travels across vast expanses of terrain, sightings by humans would be infrequent. By acquiring a territory, the Dogman would be able to regulate its food consumption and defend itself against other predators, thus being able to survive in a tough environment. This would also provide the Dogman with a sense of security and stability, thus being able to live well in its forest habitat.

We know each species has a job to perform in its environment, which is to do something particular to keep the world in balance and diverse. So, what would the Dogman do? Would it be an apex predator, a scavenger, or something else entirely?

If the Dogman is a predator, then it would require a steady supply of prey to sustain itself on. Deer are common in great numbers throughout North America. This would make them a natural source of food for such a large, carnivorous creature as the Dogman. Hunting, though, would be a difficult endeavor, particularly in killing large prey on a regular basis. Wolves, for instance, hunt in packs to kill larger animals. But it seems the Dogman would be a lone hunter, depending on their intelligence and ability to adapt and compensate for its low numbers. Here, they would likely be unable to feed themselves on a regular basis and would therefore have more of a scavenging diet.

Scavenging would be a viable alternative for the Dogman, enabling it to bully and brute its way into stealing kills from other predators. Similar to hyenas, the Dogman would be able to use its intelligence and ability to find weak or injured prey and capitalize on it. It could even steal kills from other predators such as wolves or bears. This is a behavior that would enable the Dogman to survive and thrive in their environment even without having to hunt large game on a daily basis.

This would make the Dogman a working population controller and regulator for the ecosystem of other animals. Wolves and bears are two big predators that keep deer populations under control. This control prevents overgrazing from happening and maintains the ecosystem in balance. The Dogman could do the same. It could control various animal populations and help maintain a healthy forest ecosystem. But we can't find any evidence of any unusual predator numbers or activity. This is only a hypothesis, and we'd need to investigate much further to be certain.

It may also be that the Dogman's place in the ecosystem would be far more intricate and complicated than predator-prey. It may be a keystone species where it has a particular and important role to play in order to keep the ecosystem in check. It may be environmentally adapted or a niche species that can thrive in the environment where other predators cannot. Whatever its function, the Dogman would be part of the overall ecosystem, and its presence would be a significant factor in maintaining the balance and diversity of the forest ecosystem.

Would a bipedal canid species be possible? In theory, yes, it would be possible, but it would take a long and improbable course of evolution. The possibility of a canine species developing upright motion is interesting, but it is a thesis that lives primarily in the hypothetical. There is no documented evidence of a canine that has ever manifested upright movement for more than several steps. And even those few cases are generally the result of training or experimentation and not as a form of natural behavior.

But it is not an impossibility to have some hidden suitable habitat. There are so many remote and inaccessible regions around the world that are hard to get to, and harder still to explore. These regions well might have some secrets to conceal, such as unseen life forms, such as a two-legged canid like the Dogman.

All the same, nature seems to always be hiding something. If we've learned anything from cryptozoology, it's that most myths do have a basis in reality. Perhaps the Dogman is no monster, but an animal we simply haven't yet categorized. Perhaps it's a species that has adapted to living in one type of environment, one suited to its specific needs and conditions. The hope that we may be underestimating a species already present among us is seductive. And also serves to show how much more there is to discover about the world around us.

CHAPTER 10
DOGMAN AND THE "WOO" FACTOR EXPLANATION

Dogman is the type of cryptid that challenges a normal classification. It is situated at the crossroads of cryptozoology, the paranormal, and the supernatural. Unlike Bigfoot, which is typically thought to be an undiscovered primate, Dogman seems to be a stranger and a more frightening entity. Eyewitness accounts give us a terrifying, wolf-like being on two legs that is a mass of fur and muscle. Easily disappearing into the shadows as if it was invisible. Its eyes blaze with an otherworldly light, a searing yellow or red that seems to pierce through the souls of those unlucky enough to look upon it. In some versions, the eyes of the Dogman are hypnotic, drawing in its prey with an inescapable force that cannot be accounted for by reason or science.

There are reports greater than just the physical accounts with a range of paranormal and supernatural phenomena pushing our understanding of the natural world. Some claim to have seen the creature teleport from location to location, its body disintegrating and reforming in a burst of light. Others speak of inexplicable vanishings, as if the Dogman has spirited away its victims to some other plane of existence. The creature's eyes are cited as the primary cause of these vanishings, their hypnotic abilities making its victims helpless against its whims. More bizarre are reports of interdimensional travel, as if the Dogman can traverse planes of existence at will.

Other researchers have connected Dogman sightings with UFO activity. This would suggest the creature could be part of some type of extraterrestrial activity. Some are convinced that the Dogman is an interdimensional creature, one that has been brought into our realm for purposes currently not fully known. Others think the creature is an agent or servant of some evil entity, one that wishes to use our world for its own nefarious means. Others have linked Dogman sightings to some people's occult activities. While some believe the creature is a product of dark magic or a failed summoning of some sort.

The more we explore into this potential alternate world of the Dogman, the more boundaries get erased between cryptozoology, the paranormal, and the supernatural. Maybe the creature is not just flesh and blood but exists on the border of our knowing. Its existence serves as a reminder that there are forces beyond our understanding at work in the world, forces that cannot be explained and challenge our own definition of reality. There is little doubt that the Dogman's existence is puzzling, regardless of whether it is a sign of impending disaster or a creature from another planet.

Perhaps the most frightening characteristic of Dogman sightings is that they seem to vanish as if into thin air, and individuals are left amazed and puzzled. Hunters, hikers, and drivers report observing the animal in one moment but losing it from view the next time around. Almost as if it never existed there in the first place. These disappearances don't seem like some crazy dash into the woods, where the creature just might perhaps hide out of sight. Rather, the Dogman simply seems to disappear, leaving behind nothing more than the faintest hint that it ever existed.

A 2015 sighting in Michigan is a spooky illustration of the phenomenon. A motorist was speeding down an empty road. The only noise was the roar of his engine and the groaning of the old vehicle's suspension. As he was rounding a curve, his headlights illuminated a huge, dog-like creature standing in the middle of the road on its hind legs. The amber eyes of the creature were fixed on him, and as he braked hard, it took a step forward, as though to leap up on top of his car. Instantly, however, it had disappeared into nothingness as if it had never been there. The witness would later attest that it appeared that the creature "glitched out of reality," a term fitting the supernatural capabilities of the Dogman.

This kind of phenomenon has convinced some to theorize that the Dogman is not a physical creature, as we know. But something that exists between other dimensions, phasing in and out of ours. Using this hypothesis, the Dogman would be a creature in quantum superposition. A creature being able to exist in several locations at once, and able to move freely from one dimension to another. This would account for how it seems to be able to vanish in an instant and then instantly reappear, seemingly at its will. And why it appears to possess supernatural powers. While this hypothesis is highly speculative, it's an interesting one for the explanation of the Dogman's strange behavior. And one that pushes us out of our box of existing knowledge of the natural world.

The next unusual phenomenon which has been attributed to the Dogman is that its eyes seem to glow. This is a feature unique to this creature compared to all other known nocturnal animals. Whereas eyes in most animals reflect light back, but many accounts identify the Dogman's eyes glowing in some sort of unearthly light with no apparent light source. The phenomenon has been observed in various settings, including rural regions where the creature is believed to roam. One rural Kentucky man reported seeing a dogman near his property in 2018, and his account is particularly chilling. He reported that the eyes of the creature glowed a deep red color with a light that seemed to cut through the darkness and into his own soul. But more horrifyingly still, he described feeling himself frozen where he was standing, as if some other force was holding him in place and not allowing him to move.

The witness recalled the event, "I wasn't scared, and I physically couldn't move." He explained how he felt, like he was watching himself from outside to his own body. This is not an isolated phenomenon. Many reports of Dogman involve the same type of paralysis or hypnosis. Paranormal investigators also believe that Dogman's stare can have some type of hypnotic or psychic qualities, like the "Oz Factor" often described in traditional UFO sightings. Such an experience involves bizarre silence, time displacement, or flat-out missing time when the creature is seen. Individuals are said to have a glassy-eyed, stunned, or bewildered look, as if their internal perception of space and time is being manipulated.

Does that mean the Dogman possesses psychic powers? This idea isn't as unfeasible as it might first appear to be. There are some researchers who subscribe to this school of thought. Where the glowing eyes of the Dogman may be indicative of its capability to influence the human mind. It is something that can be accomplished by utilizing a type of psychic energy or perhaps a type of telepathy. While these remain only speculation, the Dogman's glowing eyes and its supposedly hypnotic stare are certainly a fascinating subject of debate. As greater and more substantial investigations are being pursued regarding these claims, there may yet be additional discoveries in the bizarre powers of the Dogman. Maybe the Dogman does have a possible connection to the paranormal.

Another unsettling characteristic often reported in Dogman sightings is the unnatural speed of the creature. Witnesses have reported the Dogman traveling at high speeds, often covering great distances in an instant. This has been reported in many locations, and the reports are often sobering in their detail. One such report comes from a security guard in Texas who was making his rounds one evening. As he shifted, he could see a large upright canine by the edge of the trees. The creature was enormous, and its eyes were glinting like hot coals in the darkness. The guard was startled but was able to recompose himself and looked away.

However, as he glanced back in his rearview mirror, he was shocked to see the Dogman standing on the opposite side of the road, almost instantly. There was no possible way it could have crossed that distance in the time it took the guard to turn around in his vehicle and look back. If there were not two distinct Dogmen, then the beast had somehow teleported from one side of the road to the other. This left the guard stunned and bewildered. This is not a onetime occurrence as many witnesses have had similar experiences. Cases where the Dogman seems to travel at impossible speeds, defying the laws of physics as we know them.

Is the Dogman using some undiscovered type of teleportation, or is it simply faster than we can even begin to understand? Teleportation seems to be science fiction's default concept at things like this. But the Dogman's apparent power of covering long distances in seconds appears to introduce a little bit of doubt regarding established reality into the mix. Is the Dogman warping time and space itself in some way so that it can move at heart-stopping speeds? Or is there some other explanation for the phenomenon? The truth is, we don't know, and the Dogman's capacity to travel at unnatural speeds is one of the most intriguing and unexplainable parts of its activity.

One more strange theory is the way in which some investigators have pointed out an interesting phenomenon. They have claimed a majority of Dogman sightings occur in regions where there is also high UFO activity. This overlap has been seen in many locations, and in my own opinion, the overlap between the two is anything but coincidental. In 1972, some campers in Wisconsin witnessed a triangular-shaped UFO hovering over some wooded land. The following night, they were stalked by a wolf-like bipedal monster that circled their camp for hours before vanishing into the night. According to witnesses, the creature was gigantic, with eyes that glowed like hot coals in the darkness. The encounter was so vivid that the campers remained traumatized and doubted their own sanity.

The same was also reported to have happened in Pennsylvania in about 1994. A man reported seeing orb like spheres hovering in the air before seeing a huge wolf-headed monster in his backyard. The creature was reported to be over 8 feet tall with razor-sharp claws and teeth. This supposedly frightened him so much that he fled from his home and never returned until the following day. When he returned the next day, he noticed unusual burn patterns on the grass, as if the creature had been surrounded by an intense heat. The burn patterns were round, and a glowing light was seen in the middle. The man was more bewildered than ever and was left with more questions than answers. This incident is among the strangest Dogman sightings I have come across.

So, what does this imply? There are some theories that the Dogman is not an Earth born creature. But rather something related to extraterrestrials or interdimensional travelers. The theory is that the Dogman is a precursor to something greater, a sign that there are otherworldly beings or creatures that exist beyond our plane of knowledge. This theory is bolstered by the fact that there are many Dogman sightings near regions that are known for having significant UFO activity. Could this be a sign the two might somehow be related? This is all conjecture, but it raises the possibility there is some connection between UFO sightings and Dogman sightings.

Could Dogman be an interdimensional creature travelling in areas of known supernatural phenomenon? Several reports suggest the Dogman appears in places where reality itself is said to be unstable. Locations known for their high strangeness, time anomalies, and disappearances. These locations are frequently described as having a feeling of disorientation and unease, as though the fabric of reality itself is stretched. It is here that the Dogman is reported to manifest his appearance having a tendency to predict a sequence of unusual and unexplainable occurrences. Some para-psychologists have put forward theories that the Dogman could be an entity from another plane of reality. One who occasionally travels over to our own via a tear or portal.

This theory would account for why the Dogman disappears without leaving a trace, its presence appearing fleeting and brief. It would also explain how the creature is able to contradict known physical laws. Traveling at high speeds and with an agility impossible for any such living creature. Second, this idea interprets the association between Dogman sightings and UFO sightings by suggesting that the creature may be a sign of extraterrestrial entities or creatures. The concept of interdimensional creatures is not new. This is commonly heard within the Skinwalker mythology of the Navajo Nation, where they talk of creatures who have the power to change forms and travel between worlds. They are considered to have supernatural powers and are normally linked to chaos and destruction.

Could the Dogman be one of these interdimensional creatures? It is an idea that is certainly interesting, and one that provokes interesting questions regarding what our reality is and whether other dimensions may even exist.

While some blame the Dogman on UFO or interdimensional activity, others propose a more sinister cause in various occult rituals and practices. There are reports of the Dogman appearing after occult rituals, especially those where spirits or entities are summoned. These rituals use symbols, ancient chants, and other types of black magic to open doors to other dimensions and realms. It seems like the people doing these ceremonies are trying to bring forth a creature from another world, and the Dogman is what they ended up with.

A disturbing anecdotal case from 2003 in Louisiana illustrates this phenomenon. A group of teenagers, fueled by curiosity and a desire for excitement, attempted to invoke a spirit using a type of old ritual. This specific ritual involved the repeating of ancient incantations, the use of candles and other symbols, and a series of elaborate gestures. The group was immediately pursued by a large, bipedal canine that appeared to come out of nowhere. The beast was said to be humongous in stature, with eyes that glowed like burning coals in the dark. One of the teenagers later said that they had "opened a door to something they shouldn't have," suggesting that the ceremony had accidentally brought the Dogman into their reality.

Is it possible that not every Dogman sighting is just coincidence, but the result of some ritual that brought them here? If there are rituals capable of calling creatures from other dimensions, then our own reality may not be as absolute as we would assume.

The Dogman phenomenon could be more than just an undiscovered bipedal canid. This intricate web of being linked with supernatural powers, UFO sightings, interdimensional theory, and occult use means that it could be more subtle and complicated. The farther we progress through the Dogman mystery, theories are created attempting to explain why it happens. And they can be anywhere from an interdimensional being wandering between ours and potentially other dimensions, to a supernatural being relating to old culture, to even a cryptid whose abilities far surpass our understanding.

CHAPTER 11
HOAXES AND PSYCHOLOGICAL FACTORS

Some myths won't die. Regardless of how many times certain cases may be debunked. They reappear in the popular consciousness, taking a deep breath and as strong as ever. Dogman could be one of them. A creature that roams the dark woods of not only the Midwest but seemingly the entire world. With unholy encounters, unexplainable howls, and enough mystery to keep the curious engaged. Truth or lie? A trick of the mind? A combination of all three, or an actual creature?

I've spent years in awe of how myths like Dogman continue to thrive in a world where science and reason should have buried them decades ago. Some people are out to manipulate for attention and money, or even both. Others are simply misinformed. And then there are some who really believe, no matter how much the evidence mounts against them. That's where things get interesting, because at some point, it's not really about whether or not Dogman is real. It's more about if we need it to be.

Dogman tales have been around since the 1800s, but most of the evidence for its existence is anecdotal at best. We know that some of the cases are pure hoaxes, clearly fabricated to mislead the public. Others can be attributed to actual cases of misidentification that got out of hand. What's so fascinating is that some people will accept such stories without question or skepticism. Even when faced with overwhelming evidence against it. The persistence of Dogman legends is a case study in human psychology in action, entangled in fear, belief, and the excitement of the unknown.

We all love to be fooled. It is an odd and fascinating part of what it means to be human. We have a relentless desire to be frightened, drawn into the darkness of not knowing. And there are others who know about this trait and completely take advantage of it. They create highly evolved deceptions that fascinate us, and they use our primitive desires to believe in the strange and unexplainable. This is surely done for nothing more than their own gain.

Consider The *Gable Film,* for example. We have already learned this black-and-white, low-resolution video came out in the mid-2000s. It featured what looked like a two-legged, giant-sized beast charging towards the camera before the movie cut to black unexpectedly. The picture was horrifying. It was so realistic that it seemed as if the creature was really just off-camera, hidden from our view and ready to attack. And for a time, everyone really thought it was the long-sought proof that the Dogman existed among us. The video was so realistic, even old-fashioned skeptics found themselves wondering if it was real.

But in the end, the truth finally came out. The entire ordeal was a hoax with a guy in a ghillie suit, some clever editing, and a little bit of manufactured intrigue. The brainchild of the hoax even confessed to the fraud, laying out the elaborate deception that had mesmerized the world. But here's the odd thing: many people didn't want to believe the confession. They would claim there was still some truth to the film. Perhaps the hoax itself was a guise for something true. This is a phenomenon which cannot be isolated to The *Gable Film* alone; it's a common thread in many hoaxes.

Hoaxes are not only committed because some people fabricate them, but they also persist because other people simply want them to be real. There is a fundamental tendency we have to believe in the extraordinary, to belong to something larger than ourselves. This trait can be a blessing and a curse in the sense that it makes us vulnerable to manipulation and deception. Beyond the *Gable Film*, there have been many other frauds. Various people have fabricated claw marks on trees, manipulated photographs, and even created fake police reports to lend credibility to their stories. There were hoaxes perpetrated for sheer tomfoolery, others being financial scams in books, bogus artifacts, and set-up speaker tours. And then there were the others who strayed off course, pranks that became nightmares, scaring people half to death over something that never existed.

The psychological impact of these hoaxes can be extensive and devastating. They can erode the trust you may have in certain institutions. They may cause unnecessary fear and panic and can even cause harm to the physical world, including you. It's important that you be critical thinkers, that you apply tests to these claims and their evidence with a good dose of skepticism. And that you confirm information before accepting it as fact. Then and only then can you prevent being misled by the nefarious actions of those who aim to mislead you.

But not all Dogman sightings are a fabrication or a product of the imagination. Most Dogman witnesses actually believe what they saw. Something not rational or known. But many more times than not, the solution is something considerably more earthy. As a result of the ability of the mind to mislead us. Our brains are programmed to recognize patterns. This is how we make sense of the world and find meaning in the mess. This creates an effect called pareidolia, where we perceive meaningful patterns or meanings that do not exist.

Take, for instance, the case of a driver on a deserted Michigan road. One night, they saw a towering figure sprint across the highway, its glowing eyes piercing through the darkness like two embers from a dying fire. Panic surged through their veins as they slammed on the brakes, their heart racing with fear. When people looked into the incident later, they realized the man probably spotted a big dog. The fog from the nearby lake and low tree branches along the road hid it. But once the witness had the Dogman in their thoughts, their mind filled in the blanks. This turned a regular animal into a meeting with a mysterious creature. The driver's mind went into overdrive. They saw the dog's actions as benevolent, its eyes shining with an eerie brightness.

This is an extremely common experience. When the proper conditions of low light, fear, or heightened state of awareness arrive, the brain warps reality and can cause the most ordinary things to seem extraordinary. The bear standing on two legs can look humanoid in form. Its posture and demeanor give it a strange familiarity but make it completely alien. Shadows of trees in the wind can create the form of a stalking monster, their black shapes seeming to move independently. The more individuals get caught up in stories of Dogman, the more likely they are to use what they have read in order to explain an unknown reality. They envision the world as a world where the concealed is just beyond the point of being observed, waiting to pounce upon the unsuspecting. This can cause a type of psychological rabbit hole, in which reality and fantasy become more and more indistinguishable.

As we move further into the realm of Dogman sightings, we find that many of these sightings are explained by the suggestibility of how our own minds operate. In order to view what we would like to perceive; our brains are pattern-hunting devices. And when we're shown stories and pictures of Dogman, our minds begin to perceive things differently. We start to notice things we wouldn't otherwise pay attention to, and our minds make things up, creating a story that's both thrilling and terrifying. It's a reminder that the way we perceive reality is always going to be filtered through our own experience and assumptions. A place where fact and fiction get blurred together.

For decades, psychologists have been studying how one's beliefs impact their perception. When expecting to see something, one's mind will fill in the blanks so that it can confirm that belief. This is generally observed in the dark or when frightened. One walking through the woods at night, already adrenaline pumping with the rumor of Dogman, may actually believe one glimpsed the creature. Despite all the proof to the contrary.

We already know the human mind is wired to find patterns, even when none exists. This trait, which has evolutionary advantages, can also lead to widespread belief in creatures like Dogman. Mass hysteria, confirmation bias, and urban legends all play major roles in keeping cryptid stories alive. But there's something powerful about collective fear. A single sighting turns into two. Then ten. Then twenty. Suddenly, an entire town whispers about the beast lurking in the woods.

This is mass hysteria and occurs when several people are experiencing a shared delusion. A few reports of sightings of the Dogman will trigger a snowballing effect, where further people will report seeing it suddenly. Panic mounts, and soon any strange sound in the woods or strange movement of animals is attributed to the creature. This has occurred with other phenomena, from UFO reports to ghosts and even demonic clowns.

Consider, for example, the instance of the Mad Gasser of Mattoon in the 1940s. It is a tale that still chills the blood of people who experienced it. The public believed someone was quietly filling houses with a deadly gas, leaving the occupants panting for breath and writhing in pain. Mattoon, a small Illinois town, was terrorized, and this fear spread like wildfire. There were reports pouring in of individuals assaulted by a hooded attacker, and the entire town was terrorized. But surprise, surprise. No attacker! No poison! No gasser! Just people's terror making it up as it went along. Many reported gassings had simple explanations, such as spilled nail polish or odors emanating from animals or local factories.

However, local newspapers printed horror stories on the alleged attacks and presented the occurrences as facts. What was uncovered during the investigation was a typical case of mass hysteria. People in the area were already primed and afraid due to a series of reported gas attacks some months before. Then it kept growing as people's imaginations ran wild with fear. They saw hooded figures lurking around the neighborhoods and on every corner. They created their own massive conspiracy where none existed.

The same type of thing can occur with cryptids, such as Dogman. Someone notices something out of the ordinary and then they talk about it. Before long, other people recall seeing strange things too. Did they really see something? Or were their memories suggestively conditioned? It's a question that's at the heart of many cryptid sightings. We're wired to recognize patterns and to make sense of the world around us. When we're exposed to something we don't know, like a compelling story or image, our brains will fill in the gaps. Thus, creating a narrative that's both convincing and terrifying.

And the internet boards, websites, and videos only fuel the fire. A blurry photo here, an over-stated sighting there, and before long, the legend grows bigger, stronger, harder to kill. Social media websites are the perfect breeding ground for cryptid legends. People post and repost stories and photos that seem to legitimize the existence of these creatures. The distinction between fact and fiction gets smaller, and before we know it, we're left with a story that's more myth than reality. The implication has gained traction, and we're left questioning what's real and what's merely something someone's imagination created.

And then there's confirmation bias, which is the tendency to look for evidence that confirms our current opinions and dismisses all else that goes against it. This psychological trick is a powerful force that makes individuals hold on to their beliefs even when the evidence is weak. If a person believes in Dogman, then each creak of the trees, each enigmatic growl, and each pair of glowing eyes at sunset become evidence for their claim. They will interpret every detail, no matter how insignificant, and use it to confirm their claim. Even where hoaxes are uncovered, the believers remain steadfast, not wanting to believe that they were deceived.

Instead, they'll reinterpret the evidence to fit their preconceived notions. They might claim that the hoax was a clever ruse, designed to distract from the "real" truth. Or they'll argue that the hoax was staged by someone who was trying to cover up the existence of Dogman. The possibilities are endless, and the believers will stop at nothing to convince themselves that their theories are correct. This is a classic example of cognitive dissonance, where people experience discomfort when confronted with information that contradicts their beliefs. To remove their unease, they'll do anything to justify their opinions even if it means overlooking or twisting the truth.

Urban legends can also be part of the Dogman story. People share these tales over time, adding to them and making them grow. The story itself is becoming more elaborate and abundant in content. A boring story of some weird incident is now a spine-chilling tale. One of government cover-ups and hushed threats. Don't mention Dogman's name, or he'll get you. The myth takes life, growing more and more expansive with every recounting, becoming ever more frightening. The stories are enriched by extras that have been included with the recounting in a desire to astound and astonish. And the listener is left gasping in fear at the bloodshed and destruction of the creature.

And so, the myth of the Dogman is enhanced more and more in the minds of people. They start to feel that the monster exists not only because they are convinced that they saw it, but also because they have heard of it. The urban legend lingers with each new generation, refining its interpretations and nuances just a little more. And so, the process continues, with Dogman's legend expanding and flourishing year by year.

Because Dogman is surrounded by dishonesty at times, there is a moral question to consider for cryptid hunting. Should people go out looking for such creatures? If so, what's their obligation to prove their findings? Some cryptid hunters pretend to be serious researchers but really ignore scientific practices for sensationalism.

A major ethical issue is the spread of misinformation. When hoaxes or misinterpretations are presented as fact, they fuel unnecessary fear and paranoia. Some people become genuinely terrified, avoiding certain areas or experiencing anxiety over an imagined threat. This is particularly problematic when hoaxes manipulate vulnerable individuals who may already struggle with anxiety or fear of the unknown.

Another issue is the potential harm to actual wildlife. Some cryptid hunters set up traps, wander into protected lands, or disturb natural habitats in their pursuit of creatures like Dogman. In their eagerness to find evidence, they may disrupt ecosystems or put themselves in danger. Ethical research means respecting the environment and acknowledging that a lack of evidence often means there is no cryptid, rather than insisting on a cover-up.

Skepticism plays a vital role in balancing enthusiasm with reason. A healthy level of doubt prevents people from falling for hoaxes or jumping to conclusions. Real scientific inquiry requires testing claims, seeking alternative explanations, and being willing to accept when the evidence does not support the existence of Dogman.

Yet, skepticism should not turn into an outright dismissal of those who believe. Some people genuinely think they have seen something unusual. Dismissing them outright only pushes them further into their beliefs. Instead, respectful dialogue and investigation can help uncover the truth behind sightings, whether they stem from hoaxes, misidentifications, psychological factors, or the real deal.

CHAPTER 12
BUILDING THE CASE AND NOTABLE RESEARCH

To begin or re-start your investigation of the Dogman is to embark on a journey where legend and fact will blur. Such a rare cryptid can make even veteran researchers have butterflies and still be filled full of wonder. Dogman is a creature that has a human body but a wolf's head. It has scared and awed many with a combination of amazement and fear that has enthralled people for millennia. As lay scientists or as Dogman researchers, it is demanded of us to document this enigma with scientific experimentation and objective research. This allows us to address the complex combination of myth, witness accounts, and unexplained phenomena that don't add up.

This is not a path for the weak; it takes courage, diligent thinking, and unwavering perseverance to dig and discover what is true, no matter how subtle or obscure. There has been the lack of a universal process in cryptid study as a whole and specifically when dealing with the Dogman that has been glaringly remiss. Inconsistent rates of Dogman sightings require stringent field guidelines to ensure the researcher's safety and data integrity. Having a universal method of gathering and data analysis allows us to create a greater body of knowledge about the elusive beast and its existence within our society.

DEVELOPING FIELD PROTOCOLS

Creating field protocols for investigations of the Dogman requires an interdisciplinary level of understanding. Drawing from the knowledge base of various disciplines ranging from biology to anthropology, psychology, and animal tracking. Before I became involved in the study of cryptids, I knew already that there was a need to bring scientific and methodical means to carry out investigations of Dogman reports. This prompted me to create guidelines in pre-expedition planning, site selection, team establishment, and data collection, which have subsequently become the foundation of the study protocols. Understand, these protocols are not all-inclusive and will vary from researcher to researcher as well as expedition to expedition, but they will help you establish a starting point.

Pre-expedition planning, even if only following up on a reported sighting, is a critical phase of the research process. This involves a thorough review of existing reports and studies on Dogman encounters. This document review not only provides some context, but it also helps in identifying patterns or hot spots of activity. Minor details like this can prove priceless in helping you make your site selection and data collection procedures. By investigating historical observations, researchers are able to build a more sophisticated understanding of the Dogman's home range, habits, and possible motives. This can also assist you in establishing potential dangers and creating procedures for how to avoid them.

When you start a new search, choosing the right site plays a key role in your planning before the expedition. You need to take a close look at how easy it is to get into the area and how safe it is, and if Dogmen could live there. This can be done by talking to locals about their own experiences. Satellite images and a quality topo map can provide you with useful information. You can use this to shape how you do your research and collect data. Getting to know the people who live there helps you understand the culture and history behind local Dogman sightings. This could help you make sense of what you find.

Team building is also included in the pre-expedition planning and comprises creating a diverse team with expertise in each of several fields. Fields like biology, anthropology, tracking, and possibly parapsychology would be some of the fields included. By assembling a team with diverse skills and outlooks, you are better equipped to attack the research from a variety of angles. This improves your ability to gather quality information about Dogman in general. It also helps to ensure that your findings are accurate and universally applicable. This cross-disciplinary framework can also help identify any potential biases and limitations in your research design.

EQUIPMENT AND TECHNOLOGY

Making sure the team is equipped with the right tools is a critical component of any Dogman research expedition. This can make the difference between a successful investigation and a futile one. The right equipment can help you collect high-quality data, ensure your safety, and navigate the challenging terrain of remote areas. For capturing any evidence, high-definition cameras, thermal imagers and sensitive audio recorders are an essential part of your equipment. These allow your team to get fine visual and audio recordings of any possible sightings. This can make the difference between being able to prove the Dogman exists and not being able to.

Night vision and thermal features are especially beneficial considering that most sightings take place at night or during the crepuscular hours. That is when Dogman's movements and hunting ability are claimed to be strongest. By providing your team members with night vision and thermal capable binoculars and cameras, you can enhance the ability of your team to gather evidence of nocturnal Dogman activity. Also, such equipment can facilitate your team in watching the habits and habitat of the Dogman in a more natural and less invasive manner. This minimizes the chances of interfering with its regular habits or perhaps endangering your team.

Environmental sensors are also an important component of your equipment. These will enable you to cross-check the environmental factors against observations. Temperature, humidity, and air pressure sensors can provide some excellent information regarding Dogman's behavior and environmental affinity. For example, if you notice the Dogman appears at times of heavy humidity or when air pressure is low, then you can change your research design based on these parameters. With awareness of the ecological conditions that any sighting of the Dogman is linked to, you are capable of refining your understanding of its behavior and its ecology.

GPS devices and communication devices are also required to ensure the security and success of your team. By giving a GPS device to every member, you will always know where the other members are. They will also be able to travel through remote areas with difficult terrain confidently. It is also vital to have good communication equipment. You should use two-way radios or satellite phones in order to communicate with each other and the base camp if you are using one. It is particularly necessary where the cell phone signal is poor. This equipment enables you to respond to emergencies in a timely manner, coordinate activity, and send back reports of your findings in real-time. Communication, of course, is vital to the success of any research expedition.

SITE PROCEDURES

When the team gets to the area, an organized approach should be taken to gain as much systematic information as possible and reduce any potential risks. Before venturing deep into the area, a full perimeter survey should be done to get information about the surrounding area. It is a thorough search for any clues that may provide evidence of a big predator or cryptid in the area. This would include unusual prints, trampled vegetation, or dead animals. By studying these indicators, you may be able to learn a great deal about the Dogman's lifestyle, home, and possible travel in that location.

One of the key aspects of the perimeter assessment is to look for signs of recent activity, such as fresh tracks, scat, or other indicators of the Dogman's presence. This can help you or your team to determine the likelihood of a sighting. It can also help in your decision on where to focus our efforts. You also need to be aware of any potential hazards in the area, such as steep slopes, fast-moving water, or other obstacles that could pose a risk to your safety.

Having quality observation posts is also something that is important in your research plan. Placing the observation posts where Dogman is purported to be moving will give you a better chance of getting any evidence. The observation posts must be placed ideally so that they offer an unobstructed view of the area. They should also reduce the chances of detection by the Dogman. Alternating shifts among members guarantee around-the-clock surveillance without exhaustion, and they can remain highly alert and watchful all day long. You might also need to factor in the weather and have different locations selected for the prevailing winds.

In the event of a sighting or encounter, it's vital to have some predetermined plans in place to ensure your safety and the integrity of any viable data collection. This includes maintaining a safe distance from the Dogman, avoiding sudden movements that might provoke it, and refraining from direct eye contact. This would be typical in any canine behavior and would most likely be perceived as a challenge. By following these protocols, you can minimize the risk of an encounter becoming aggressive or confrontational. This will also ensure that you can collect any valuable data from the observed dogman.

Your interaction and communication protocols also call for a series of other precautions to protect your and your team's safety and the success of the expedition. These are things like carrying bear spray or other deterrents. Wearing protective gear and other equipment and being prepared to move back to a safe location if there is a problem. You can lower your risk of a Dogman or other wild animal attack. You can also steer clear of harm from the surroundings by thinking ahead about different scenarios. This will also boost your odds of getting solid information.

DOCUMENTING THE DATA

Detailed documentation is the foundation of all accurate research, and it is necessary that it be kept to a high standard of detail and precision throughout your expedition. A field journal may be the most important resource for keeping a record of our observations, reflections, and any irregularities encountered during the expedition as they happen. A journal should be kept and recorded daily by each member of the team. It is a tool to document your experience, look for patterns and trends, and correlate unique pieces of evidence. This can be something written on paper, electronic, or a combination of both. It comes down to your or the team's personal preference.

In addition to field journals, most research groups also rely heavily on photographic evidence to capture images of tracks, possible shelters, or any other physical evidence that may be relevant. When taking photographs, it's essential to include some kind of scale (such as a ruler or a common object) to help with size estimation during analysis. I like to use a dollar bill as it is approximately 6″x2.5″. This can be useful when evaluating the size and shape of tracks or other physical evidence. By including a scale in the photograph, you can ensure that your measurements are accurate and reliable. This is critical when making conclusions about the Dogman's behavior and habitat.

Any documentation process also requires proper sampling. That includes the collection of hair samples, scat, or dirt taken from impression-bearing areas for lab analysis. If it is safe and possible, you would also sample other biological specimens, such as saliva or tissue samples, to possibly get DNA evidence or biological data. As we have previously discussed, this would be a definite way to establish Dogman as a species. It would also provide any potential genetic relationship with other animals, and their behavior and environments.

When taking samples, there need to be proper procedures set in place to guarantee that the samples are handled and stored properly. This involves the use of sterile equipment, labeling the samples correctly, and keeping them safe so that they are not lost or contaminated. With these procedures, you can guarantee that your samples will be of high quality. This will help us learn a lot about the biology and the ecology of the Dogman.

Along with using field journals, photographs, recordings, and samples, researchers often use other pieces of equipment for documentation. These may include items like audio tape recordings, witness video clips, and witness verbal or written reports. These can offer a better view of what they have found and may enable them to determine any possible patterns or trends. By keeping good documentation and using the various tools and techniques currently available, they are able to ensure that their research remains credible and reliable.

DATA ANALYSIS & REPORTING

After returning from the field, the actual work begins, and this a critical phase of the research process. Data collation is only the first step. This is where you bring together all the observations, recordings, and samples for comprehensive analysis. This cooperative method means that all detail is documented, and you can observe any potential trends and patterns which may have otherwise remained unseen during the expedition. As you collate data from the diverse sources, you can gain better in-depth insight into the biology, habitat, and behavior of the Dogman.

In order to make sure that your findings are true and reliable, invite experts from various fields to review the results of the data which was collected. For example, a wildlife biologist can distinguish between known animal tracks and possible cryptid tracks. Similarly, a geneticist may do DNA testing on the samples to give you the genetic make-up and any other correlation of the Dogman with any known animal to eliminate them. And a geologist can tell you the geological background of the area and give you potential habitats. You need expert analysis to classify not only the Dogman but any new species.

I mean, expert opinion is required in whatever research you conduct. And it enables you to draw from a pool of knowledge that can examine and critique your findings. This is to be done by collaborating with experts who are in fields related to the data gathered. Your research can then be classified as valid and rigorous. And what you are left with as a result is a thorough understanding of the Dogman. This kind of collaborative effort could also create a sense of community and shared understanding. I think we should all work together to construct our knowledge of this mysterious animal.

Once you have done your analysis and interpretation of the data, it is essential that you circulate the findings with the wider research world via conferences, journals, or the web. This is a critical part of the research process, where one may make the findings available and invite others' constructive criticism. When researchers share their results, it helps promote cooperation as well as further knowledge beyond our current understanding of the Dogman. We also need to engage the public with education and outreach efforts. It is critical to introduce the public to the importance of cryptid research and the potential usefulness of information about such elusive or thought to be extinct animals.

Reporting and publication are critical parts of any research endeavor. These require the highest level of accuracy and commitment to accuracy and transparency. Sharing the results with the broader research community enables us to have our research thoroughly tested and ensures all the findings are evidence-based.. This collective approach also offers additional contributions to the existing body of knowledge regarding the Dogman and where it is at today in the natural world. This collaboration will also help build the foundation for additional research and investigation.

NOTABLE RESEARCH

Many dedicated organizations and individuals have emerged in the quest to explain the Dogman phenomenon, and their studies have been essential to comprehending this enigmatic being. The North American Dogman Project (NADP), founded by Joedy Cook, a former member of the U.S. Army and Iraq War veteran, is one of the most well-known. Cook's career change from military life to cryptid investigation was fueled by an enthusiasm to unearth the mysteries of America's backcountry. The NADP has a mission: to compile as much data on the Dogman phenomenon as is available. Through organizing, networking, researching, and reporting, the organization has established a platform for enthusiasts and researchers to collaborate, giving a systematic and comprehensive approach to reporting Dogman.

Another group which has contributed significantly to the investigation of Dogman is the Virginia Dogman Research (VDR), which also turns out to be a chapter of the NADP. The VDR has experience with regional research in Virginia and draws from an eclectic pool of membership. They are composed of ex-military personnel, lawmen, and veteran cryptozoological researchers. This diverse group of expertise and experience provides richness to their investigating methods and credibility to their results. With their combined experience, the VDR has been able to manage challenging cases and introduce a greater understanding of the Dogman phenomenon.

Linda S. Godfrey was another renowned author and researcher in the quest of Dogman. She cut her teeth on this enigmatic creature writing the first accounts of the Beast of Bray Road. Godfrey had researched dog-like cryptid myths and sightings significantly for over 30 years. She put accounts of werewolves and similar such tales as far back as the late 1700s in the public eye. She put present-day observations into context historically and has popularized the phenomenon of Dogman into mainstream knowledge. Unfortunately, Linda Godfrey passed away on November 27, 2022. But her commitment has opened the field to so many, and her research has contributed to progress in the field of the Dogman.

Collaboration is the lifeblood of cryptid research, and Dogman missions are no exception. Through working together, sharing information, resources, and knowledge, researchers can approach the Dogman enigma from every angle, increasing the possibility of success. One of the most well-known cooperative endeavors was in Elkhorn, Wisconsin, researching the Beast of Bray Road. Various researchers headed up Linda S. Godfrey, teamed up to hunt for proof of a wolf-like creature running around the Bray Road area. Through fieldwork, interviews, and media outreach, the team brought national publicity to the phenomenon. This, in turn, prompted further witnesses to emerge and with them, the then-current evidence base grew.

The North American Dogman Project has also conducted many regional investigations. They have put together a team of experts in a very broad range of fields. Their investigations involved careful planning, from reviewing previous sighting reports to using the latest monitoring equipment in established hotspots. This team effort ensures the thorough approach with fieldwork merged with data examination to authenticate or disprove observed encounters. Together, they can pool their resources and avoid the limitations of single research and get closer to a holistic view of this phenomenon we are calling Dogman.

Besides participating in physical excursions, researchers have also turned to the web to gain firsthand accounts, beliefs, and opinions. This helps them gain knowledge and reports from a broader base of both Dogman witnesses and skeptics. By sending questionnaires and joining web forums on platforms such as Reddit, they have reached a huge cache of anecdotal data. Which has provided a better understanding of the extent to which the Dogman phenomenon occurs on an international scale and the various cultural interpretations that it has manifested under.

Entering the field of Dogman research will put you on a path of doubt, hope, and always the persistent challenge of sorting facts from fantasy. Through the creation and usage of strong field procedures, collaborating with other dedicated researchers, and adopting collaborative research paradigms, researchers can escape the constraints of solo-study models and gain an increased understanding of this mysterious creature. As we venture into the puzzle that is Dogman, we must anchor ourselves with rigorous questions and skeptical examination. We must also be willing to prove oneself wrong for this very exercise; only in that way will we have an element of chance to unravel this mystery surrounding Dogman. Therefore, shedding a much-needed light on so many pending questions about this creature.

CHAPTER 13
TECHNOLOGICAL FRONTIERS IN DOGMAN RESEARCH

Cryptid science is revolutionizing. That which was long written off as myth and legend has gained a new degree of credibility, simply due to the increasingly fast-paced speed of technology. One of the many cryptids to find itself in the focus of scientists, amateur researchers, and skeptics is the mysterious Dogman. The wolf-like bipedal creature is said to be seen and reported by many witnesses from around the world. It appears mainstream scientific communities are reluctant and slow to embrace such beings. However, independent scientists and some unbiased experts are exploiting the power of sophisticated tools to investigate these assertions.

The largest contributor of the past few decades has been the emergence of artificial intelligence (AI), machine learning, and expanding DNA databases. This has totally revolutionized cryptid research by allowing researchers to cross-check data in ways that previously were not available. Not only has this technology changed the more efficient gathering and analysis of evidence, but the ability to catch patterns and links not seen before. Additionally, the standardizing of data gathering and analysis has enabled average individuals to create informative findings and conclusions, thus revolutionizing the study of cryptids.

Citizen science has played an important role in this revolution as well by enabling the participation of people from all walks of life. This helps the research process by providing additional help with the data collection. This process not only increased the scope of the research but also created an atmosphere of belonging and common purpose among researchers and enthusiasts. So, the study of Dogman is no longer anecdotal but a science with quantifiable outcomes, where on the basis of facts inferences are made and hypotheses can be tested.

This collaboration between technology and public engagement has also opened up new avenues of exploration. Devices that involve the use of acoustic sensors, camera traps, and other novel means of sensing and monitoring potential Dogman sightings. Advances in AI-augmented analysis tools have allowed scientists to rummage through vast data stores. Quickly finding patterns and irregularities which can point to a greater phenomenon. As the field continues to evolve, we will one day be able to see a deeper understanding of the Dogman and other cryptids. An understanding based on empirical evidence and uncompromising scientific inquiry.

THE ROLE OF AI

Using artificial intelligence (AI) now allows researchers to examine photographs and footage with never-before-seen accuracy. By using these deep-learning algorithms, they can now filter through a vast compilation of images in a matter of seconds. Those images can then be cross-checked against master sets of documented wildlife to sift out misidentifications and minimize possible human error. This fresh approach allows researchers to focus on the most intriguing and inexplicable occurrences rather than spending time on those which can be explained.

For instance, machine learning software is trained to identify from extensive sets of wolves, bears, and big dogs and can distinguish between these wild animals and potential anomalies with precision. Scanning through thousands of photographs in a matter of seconds and finding patterns and characteristics that can verify the presence of an unfamiliar or unidentified animals. If a photograph shows characteristics incompatible with documented forms, the system flags it for further examination. This guarantees that researchers spend most of their time on the most captivating and potentially cryptid-related investigations. Not only does this save time but guarantees unsubstantiated theory is not converted to conclusions, thus making the research empirical.

Aside from the analytical side of AI software is the capacity in different applications to improve poor-quality films. This can aid researchers in uncovering hidden facts and disclosing otherwise obscured details. With AI, investigators are now able to eliminate distortions, correct light, and retrieve lost data. They now have the capability of turning grainy, pixelated pictures into sharp, high-definition images. This method is already being successfully used in forensic science and is now on its way to being used in cryptid research. Offering the investigator a new, very useful tool to break out when investigating and analyzing strange videos.

One of the scariest elements of the Dogman phenomena is it howls. Many of the witness reports include hearing low grunts, foreboding howls, or guttural noises. To sort out these bizarre noises, researchers are now looking at AI-powered sound analysis technology. They can use this to cross-reference the recordings with known animal sounds and look for anomalous patterns. Bioacoustic AI software was initially intended to monitor whale calls and bird songs. By reusing software such as this, researchers are now able to use these programs today in the investigation of Dogman.

This advanced audio analysis tool can detect the minute pitch, tone, and frequency changes. These may uncover any recorded voice patterns not known to be present in existing species. Acoustic parameter analysis of such recordings will allow the scientists to detect the patterns and signatures that can guide them towards an unfamiliar species like Dogman. For instance, Bioacoustic AI can analyze a sound's frequency spectrum, amplitude, and spectral content. With this, investigators can extract some characteristics which can set it apart from known animal calls.

Using the sound analysis with artificial intelligence in Dogman investigations has provided new areas for research that allow researchers to investigate the auditory aspect of these mysterious creatures. By cross-matching reported sounds made during Dogman sightings against a vast database of animal vocalizations, researchers can determine potential anomalies. These anomalies can be taken as circumstantial evidence of the creature's existence. This approach has the potential to revolutionize our understanding of Dogman, presenting us with a new paradigm to learn about their behavior and communication ability.

Cutting through anomaly detection and analysis of visual and auditory evidence is just one aspect of AI. It can also be used on the vast database of sighting report information that can be correlated with dogman. With this kind of information in such a system, researchers are able to identify patterns and relationships that may have been obscure to researchers because of human variables. AI-powered computer analysis of sighting reports, for instance, can identify patterns in time, place, and witness descriptions and provide important clues about the creature's range and activities.

For most researchers, probably the greatest strength of this kind of methodology is the ability to determine possible hot spots for follow-up investigations. Geographic coordinates and descriptions given for alleged sightings can be processed by AI to determine areas where the creature is likely to be seen. This might include determining groups of sightings over specific geography, such as thick forests, rivers, or mountains. Or it can expose patterns when the sightings occur, showing that Dogman is active in a particular month or at a particular time of day or in a particular place.

Interpreting eyewitness testimony using AI also makes it easier to decide on specific creature descriptions that would be more common in certain areas. For instance, AI can reveal that the witnesses at a specific location are likely to describe the creature in terms of having a unique coat pattern. Or maybe even some unique arrangement of body features. By identifying such patterns and trends, researchers are more likely to accumulate useful evidence to define Dogman as a species. For example, an AI system would be capable of recognizing that sightings are likely to be made by people with knowledge of the area or experience in wildlife observations. By realizing these inconsistencies and biases of different sightings, scientists are able to have a better hold of the information and make the result more credible.

EDNA AND DATABASES

Cryptozoology and Dogman studies have been foiled for decades by a failure to provide physical evidence from any form of genetic testing. Despite hopes that hair, saliva, or scat samples would be the solution to discovering a Dogman species, most forms of such samples have been eliminated. This is based on the non-availability of comparative samples. That is being changed with the newer forms of genetic analysis, databases and particularly Environmental DNA (eDNA).

Environmental DNA is a revolutionary tool that allows researchers to collect genetic materials from soil, water, or air samples. This new process does not require the physical specimen. This approach has already been used to confirm the presence of various rare species in remote areas, and it is now being tested in Dogman investigations. For Dogman research, this means that a footprint, a disturbed riverbank, or even a tree where a creature reportedly scratched it could hold genetic evidence. By analyzing these samples, scientists can determine whether the recovered DNA matches known species or something unknown.

Using eDNA in Dogman research is a huge step forward. This enables scientists to get genetic material where the animal is suspected to have passed. It has the potential to be a game-changer in cryptid science. It gives science a new method for detecting and identifying an unknown species. eDNA analysis can also be used to investigate the behavior and ecology of not just Dogman but other cryptids as well. This could provide insightful information regarding their habits and habitats.

But the issue with Dogman DNA testing has always been there is no control DNA material to reference. When the genetic sample does not match what is in the file, it generally gets eliminated as "inconclusive." But as the DNA databases grow, more and more species are being included, with less room for misidentification. Many of the newer databases include ancient DNA sequences, with a greater idea of what extinct species might have surviving relatives. This is important to hypotheses proposing cryptids such as Dogman could be surviving populations of prehistoric animals that were thought to have become extinct.

Suppose, for instance, that a genetic sample is half-a-match for an animal such as the extinct dire wolf or an unknown canid species. This would be a gigantic step in the classification process. This would imply that the Dogman could be a living member of a species previously believed to be extinct, or a new species entirely. The implications of such a discovery would be staggering. It would challenge our current understanding of evolution and the diversity of life on Earth. And as we construct and create these databases of DNA, we can expect more revelations in the science of Dogman research, and indeed even new species.

One of the most exciting developments in the field of cryptid and Dogman research is the emergence of affordable, portable DNA testing kits. Traditionally, genetic analysis required expensive lab work, which limited its accessibility to independent researchers. However, with the advent of new field kits, researchers can now extract DNA samples with relative ease.

Some of these portable DNA testing kits have revolutionized the field of Dogman research. They have enabled researchers to collect and analyze genetic material in the field, rather than relying on laboratory-based analysis. This not only saves time and resources but also allows researchers to respond quickly to new sightings and collect valuable data in real-time. The kits are also relatively affordable, making them accessible to researchers who may not have had the budget for traditional laboratory-based analysis. The downside to this analysis is they are based only on current databases, which can provide a lot of "unknown" results.

But some of the Dogman and other cryptid investigation groups have worked with professional laboratories to make their work credible and verifiable. Rather than sending samples to private companies with undisclosed agendas, these groups collaborate with geneticists who are open to looking for alternative explanations of what they find. This collaboration not only adds credibility to their efforts but also guarantees that any meaningful anomalies are tested and checked within the accrediting institutions.

With the help of such expert laboratories, the researchers can now be sure that their results are thoroughly verified and validated. And on sound scientific reasoning, removing any speculation to the conclusions regarding the data. It also provides ways of accessing more forms of genetic analysis methods and tools, which can yield higher accuracy and precision of information for the genetic content in question.

Second, the advent of portable DNA testing kits and collaborative working with professional laboratories has also allowed researchers to address some of the criticism of Dogman research. Things such as a lack of peer review and contamination or misidentification of samples. By collaboratively working with established labs and the application of established protocols for genetic testing, researchers can guarantee that their results are valid and worthy of scientific consideration.

INTEGRATING CITIZEN SCIENCE

The field of Dogman research has experienced a revolution over the last few years with the arrival of new technology and the increasingly active involvement of ordinary people. Cryptid study was once composed of individual researchers working on the fringes, often dependent on witness accounts and shoestring budgets. But since the arrival of smartphones, drone technology, and worldwide data-sharing websites, the study of Dogman has been revolutionized.

Another key development in Dogman research is the emergence of crowdsourcing. This allows witnesses to post real-time testimony, upload pictures, video, and any location data to the internet. This brings with it several benefits, not least being the location history of events, cutting down on the possibility of false reports. It also means analysts can crossmatch the evidence, observing if many unrelated witnesses report similar experiences. These mass data sets are another thing which can be searched for trends by AI.

Sites such as the North American Dogman Project (NADP) already maintain records and provide an open-source platform for researchers to collaborate and contribute data. However, more recently developed systems are capable of filtering and geolocation reports automatically to review, painting a clearer picture of Dogman sightings. These also highlight the general concentration points for most reports, so researchers know where to prioritize investigation and further input.

Citizen scientists are also taking part in Dogman research, performing aerial surveys across remote areas with drones in order to gather data on wildlife populations. Thermal imaging drones, previously limited to wildlife monitoring, can photograph forests at sunset and pick up warm signatures that would indicate massive unknown creatures. Sometimes these drones have captured unexplainable movement, whether or not they are phony reports, hoaxes, or actual Dogman sightings, they remain suspect. But what is certain is that technology is enabling the law enforcement to patrol distant areas with an effectiveness that would have been impossible a decade ago.

Using drones with remote sensing technologies has also provided new opportunities for research. They are allowing researchers to observe dogman habitats and activity patterns more intensively. Satellites and drones provide data that can be used to determine patterns and trends in dogman activity and create more efficient methods of detecting and tracking the creatures.

Overall, the growing participation of everyday people in Dogman research, and the creation of new technology, is the answer to unlocking the subject. This will help in illuminating the behavior and nature of the creature in new ways. With scientists continuously inventing and refining instruments and techniques, we can expect to see a dramatic improvement in the quantity and quality of observations obtained. And thus, an improved understanding of the enigmatic Dogman.

Although much has been accomplished in the study of Dogmen, mainstream science remains to be skeptical. And most mainstream researchers are suspicious, if not contemptuous, of cryptid research. But history teaches us that skepticism does not always mean impossibility. There are many instances of animals that were once thought mythical or exaggerated but were later found to exist through scientific investigation.

With integrating AI and expanding DNA databases, along with the rise of citizen science, we are forcing a shift in the way that mainstream scientists approach dogman research. These advancements have provided researchers with the tools and techniques necessary to investigate unknown creatures in a more rigorous and systematic way. Additionally, the expansion of DNA databases is providing researchers with a wealth of genetic information that can be used to identify and classify unknown species.

The growth of citizen science is now playing an important role in the development of Dogman studies. By including the public in the scientific community, researchers have the ability to gain data information from a more diverse source. This will ultimately help to prove or refute Dogman sightings. Citizen science initiatives, like the North American Dogman Project, are bridging the divide of data exchange between researchers and the public and creating a more complete picture of Dogman activity.

The future of Dogman study is not blurry pictures or crazy campfire tales, but in hard data, high-level analysis, and greater reliance on technology. The more technologies and methods we employ, the closer we come to actual answers, whatever they ultimately turn out to be. Whether a Dogman does or does not exist, fresh approaches are being developed in cryptid science. These will provide more precision on how we carry on the quest for mysterious creatures and challenge the institutions of science. Possibly to be more detached in their reaction rather than dismissing the anomalies. By adopting the approach and equipment of modern science, we are able to step away from myth and conjecture and towards a more realistic, fact-based reality model of the world.

Finally, the hunt for Dogman is not so much about discovering a mythical creature as it is about discovering the limits of our understanding and knowledge of the natural world. By pushing the limits of what we thought was possible, we might be able to discover new species, new habitats, and new insight into the behavior and biology of animals. Dogman investigation teaches us that science is infinite in seeking and discovery. And even the most seemingly impossible assertions sometimes prove to be true if the right tools and equipment are in one's hands.

CHAPTER 14
BRIDGING SCIENCE AND CRYPTOZOOLOGY

Humans are fascinated by enigmas. That's why folklore keeps going, urban legends grow, and tales of mysterious creatures never really die. Among the cryptids rumored to inhabit our planet, few inspire the same spontaneous response as Dogman. There is something to the notion of a half-man, half-wolf creature that strikes a primordial chord, summoning an inherent fear that's difficult to overcome. Perhaps it's our ancient fear of predators, the one that has been etched into our collective psyche for millennia. Perhaps it's the eerie way witnesses report it moving, unnatural and foreboding, something that's just wrong and can't be explained.

Unlike Bigfoot, typically thought to be a reclusive and shy giant, Dogman is another type completely. The sightings are typically reported as more violent. A creature that does not seem to avoid human interaction and will even attack humans sometimes, leaving them terrified and confused. Dogman has been reported by some witnesses as walking upright on two legs, with a body covered in black, matted fur, with eyes that glow like embers at night. Others say that it is like a wolf with a human, deformed face and razor-claws. Real or misidentifications of well-known animals notwithstanding, one fact is sure: Dogman has established a niche in contemporary mythology, fascinating people across the globe.

But we know mythology alone isn't enough to convince the scientific community. Science demands some kind of proof. Some type of physical evidence, repeatable results, and a rigorous process that eliminates alternative explanations. That's where the divide begins. Cryptozoologists, the researchers and enthusiasts hunting for creatures like Dogman, face an uphill battle. Mainstream scientists are suspicious of the cryptozoologist's efforts, even outright dismissive at times. Many regard it as a fringe field and pseudoscience that's more concerned with sensation than rigorous investigation. And for good reasons, cryptozoology has a long history of sensationalism, from hoaxes to misidentifications. These are the things which have discredited the field and made it more difficult for serious researchers to be heard.

Even mainstream scientists cannot close their eyes to the reality that there are creatures that were previously believed to be myths and legends such as the mountain gorilla or okapi. Each of these was eventually discovered and suddenly became real. The legend of the mountain gorilla was busted during the 19th century, and the giraffe-like okapi was discovered in the early 20th century. These discoveries affirm that the most unlikely beings do indeed exist, and that our perception of reality is not absolute. The question becomes then, what will it take to consider such creatures as Dogman? Would it take some form of physical proof, like a body or skeleton? Will anecdotal evidence finally add up to be enough? Whatever the response may be, there is no doubt: the search for Dogman and other cryptids will continue, driven by our hunger to understand our world.

At its core, science is about discovery. But it's also about the process. Evidence must be testable, observable, and repeatable. When it comes to cryptids, the problem is that evidence is almost always anecdotal. Eyewitness accounts, blurry photos, and strange sounds in the night don't seem to cut it. People misremember, exaggerate, or sometimes just outright lie. And without a body, a skeleton, or even DNA evidence, scientists have little reason to invest resources into a search. The lack of concrete evidence is a major obstacle in the search for cryptids like Dogman, and it's a problem that has plagued the field of cryptozoology for decades.

There is also the question of association. Cryptozoology attracts not only serious researchers but also hoaxers and conspiracy theorists. Like the notorious 2008 Georgia Bigfoot hoax, when two men Matt Whitton and Rick Dyer reported they had discovered the body of a Bigfoot in northern Georgia. They showed the body as a frozen furry corpse, and they agreed to give DNA evidence and pictures to prove that it actually existed. It then came out that the body had been a rubber gorilla costume stuffed with animal guts and frozen. When real researchers get mixed up with hoaxers, it becomes too simple to dismiss their work. The media then hypes cryptozoology as a mystery science that is all about entertainment, not scientific study. And when the general public regards cryptozoology as a joke, it's more difficult for real researchers and their work to be respected.

But we know that science is not completely shut off from the possibility of undiscovered species. The finding of the coelacanth, the fish which was believed to have gone extinct 66 million years ago, shows that there are holes in what we think we know. The giant squid was once a sailor's tall tale and was finally filmed by scientists in 2012. Even today, new species continue to be found in deep-sea trenches and inaccessible rainforests. But the truth is, these animals left behind some kind of physical evidence. Take the case of the coelacanth, for instance, which was rediscovered in 1938 when a live specimen was hauled in off the coast of South Africa. The giant squid, however, was imaged by a team of scientists in 2012, giving definitive evidence of its existence.

For Dogman or any other cryptid to be accepted, the evidence needs to be irrefutable. But how do you prove the existence of something that may not want to be found? It's a chicken-and-egg problem: without evidence, scientists are unlikely to invest resources in a search, but without a search, it's unlikely that evidence will be found. It is my belief the answer can indeed be found through a more scientific approach to cryptozoology. One that uses tested scientific methods, technological advances, and paradigm advances in research. Through coordination of efforts and resources and sharing of information, researchers might come up with improved ways of finding and studying cryptids. But until they can do so, finding Dogman and other cryptids will prove hard and most often contentious.

The first step towards the evolution of cryptozoology is to shift its focus away from being pseudoscience to actual research. That includes adopting scientific rigor and not trying to push it away. Cryptozoology must adopt correct methodologies, such as wildlife tracking instruments, DNA analysis, and forensic tracking procedures. A methodical approach to gathering evidence instead of relying on folklore and hearsay material. In this way, scientists can establish a solid foundation for their research and be most likely to achieve a breakthrough.

Among the rapidly developing and most promising research areas is that of using forensic methods and physical samples. DNA testing, footprints, hair samples, and scat can yield actual breakthroughs in the hunt for Dogman. In many instances where unexplained biological material has been encountered, lab tests yield "unknown primate" or a mix of a recognizable animal DNA. But the problem here can be contamination if most of the samples are not collected properly or are dropped. Proper research practice would be to not use those types of samples and get verifiable samples under tight control. Such as through the use of sterilized apparatus and limiting human interaction with the environment. In this manner, scientists are able to increase the likelihood of producing plausible results and lowering false positives.

Another important facet of cryptozoology would be interdisciplinary cooperation. Rather than being solo operators, researchers need to work with experts in genetics, zoology, and anthropology. When experts from various disciplines work together, the integrity of the inquiry increases, and opportunities for discovering something worthwhile rise. A Dogman expedition supported by biologists and forensic experts is more credible than one done by enthusiasts only. For instance, a group of experts in DNA analysis can identify the genetic structure of an enigmatic sample. And a zoologist can tell you a lot about the animals' habits and environment.

Using modern technology is also becoming increasingly important in cryptozoology. Since the arrival of smartphones, drones, and motion-sensitive cameras, it is now easier than ever to gather information. Whatever odd creature roams the woods, camera traps should get it, eventually. Thermal imagers are able to detect big, warm-blooded animals such as Dogman even deep within forests. A well-organized expedition, with the use of all available technology, would stand a much greater chance of producing results than anecdotal testimony. For example, a series of camera traps can be used in a specific area to track animal movement. Then thermal imaging can be used to identify heat signatures in the environment.

Skepticism plays too minor a role in cryptozoology. In a tragic irony, the most effective way to make cryptozoology sound credible is to doubt false reports. The farther away from hoaxes researchers move, the more convincing their argument becomes. If an unexplained howl in the forest is merely a coyote with an unusual vocal cord, admitting it does not discredit the field, it strengthens it. Science lives on skepticism, and so should cryptozoology. By being skeptical and rigorous, researchers can establish a sound foundation for their research and have a higher likelihood of devising meaningful results.

Skepticism does not mean dismissing everything at face value. That's what cynics and deniers do. It's being critical of claims, demanding evidence, all the while keeping oneself open to unknown possibilities. The best scientists are those that don't assume they already know it all but instead approach each new discovery with a healthy dose of curiosity and humility. And after all, history is filled with things once thought impossible, only to be true. Dr. Mireya Mayor's finding of the mouse lemur is a case in point. This small primate had never before been recorded by science. A new species of mouse lemur, the world's smallest primate, was found by Mayor and her team of researchers in 2000 while they were studying the forests of Madagascar. This finding validated the fact that even in an expertly studied and satellite-mapped world, there are still new and elusive animals that could continue to hide in the shadows and await discovery.

At the same time, blind acceptance of anything is as lethal as blind rejection. Whoever accepts every bizarre story they are presented with will only lower themselves. That is why cryptozoologists must be their own worst critics. If the goal is to prove that there is a beast like Dogman, then the evidence must be strong enough to survive the most severe criticism. Otherwise, it's another spooky story, a myth that lacks any foundation in reality. The search for truth calls for a demand for tough testing and scrutiny, not a readiness to accept everything that seems interesting or convincing.

Others would argue that the hunt is everything, and the mystery is the real draw. They believe that Dogman and other cryptids are more powerful as myth than as facts of science. But isn't the search for the truth more intriguing? What if, one day, there was undeniable proof that surfaced? A living specimen, or skeletal remains, or even a corpse. This would be a discovery that realigned what we believed was possible. The possibility of finding such a creature as Dogman, a creature whose existence has obsessed human minds for centuries, is an enticing suggestion. It would be a finding that would rebuild our understanding of the natural world and create a new generation of scientists and explorers into the world.

Science, myths, and folklore don't have to be at odds. They can exist in harmony while complimenting each other. The unknown should be explored, but it must be done with clear eyes and sharp minds. Because if Dogman is out there, we owe it to ourselves to find out the truth. We have a duty to those who've dedicated their lives to finding answers. We have an obligation to the researchers who've devoted themselves to gain knowledge. And we have a responsibility for the curious public about what this discovery might bring. By pushing ahead with a good amount of doubt and a dedication to research based on facts, we can figure out what's going on, one way or the other.

AFTERWORD

In this book, we have followed the intricate dance between scientific investigation and Dogman legend, a mystery that has intrigued and captivated us for centuries. Eyewitness testimony, historical accounts, and cryptozoological research all point to a residual presence of something out of the ordinary lurking in the shadows. Scientific explanations try to account for these sightings in terms of psychology, misidentifications, and the existence of unknown species. The proximity of folklore teeming with legend, fear, and cultural meaning and with scientific inquiry is simultaneously trying to underscore the limitations of our current knowledge. And to testify to the profound human impulse to make the intelligible the inexplicable.

The Dogman phenomenon has captivated individuals of all cultures and throughout history, generating controversy, rumor, and new questions. As we persist in our quest for the secrets of this enigmatic creature, we are reminded of the diversity and richness of human existence. The Dogman is a boundary between the known and the unknown, a boundary that we constantly keep returning to, like moths to a flame. Apart from whatever we may want to believe about the Dogman as a folkloric being or as a symbolic figure for our ultimate nightmare and desire, its existence in our collective imagination cannot be denied.

But even so, whatever it is, the mystery remains. The Dogman phenomenon continues to burst with new photos and video, spurring debates, and demanding investigation. Ever-increasing progress in technology and ways of investigating will inevitably leave no stone unturned. And then, somehow or other, we will most likely discover undeniable proof or a sensible explanation for these phenomena. Until this is achieved, the urge to pursue it cannot be over-exaggerated. Each study, each report, each analysis instructs us not only about Dogman, but about fear, belief, and the unknown in general. By examining the nature of this phenomenon, we may better understand ourselves and our place in the world.

What makes us keep looking? Is it perhaps the same impulse that has motivated man for centuries: the pursuit of truth? We must find answers to things that cannot be explained. We have a desire to know more than we believe we know. The legend of the Dogman persists because it resonates with our primitive nature. A terror of the darkness, a fear of the untamed, and awe. The awe at beasts that might roam outside of our human understanding. Whatever the Dogman is, an undiscovered species, a common human psychological phenomenon or something in between. The hunt will continue so long as there are people who will look. The mystery may never be resolved, but maybe that makes it so inescapable.

The Dogman phenomenon is now part of our shared common cultural heritage. Is it a product of human imagination and the necessity to believe in something one does not know? It became the source of inspiration for many works of art, books, and songs, and part of our shared common cultural heritage. With our quest for Dogman's secrets, we remember the value of curiosity, the value of asking questions, and the value of seeking answers. The hunt for the Dogman is a hunt for oneself. A reminder, there is always something new to discover, something new to learn, and something new to dig up in this wide, wide world of ours.

SUMMARIZING THE SCIENTIFIC FINDINGS AND FOLKLORE

Scientific investigation of the Dogman sightings has brought forth a great variety of theories regarding the phenomenon's source. Sightings, in most skeptics, opinions are misidentifications of known animals such as large wolves, bears, or feral exotic pets. Existing animals wrongly identified as the mysterious Dogman. The role of pareidolia, a mental phenomenon whereby the mind perceives what seems like familiar shapes, such as faces or figures, cannot be ruled out. Perceptual bias may lead witnesses to perceive normal events as abnormal events, primarily as a result of social and cultural expectation. For instance, a person with a good background in myth and folklore would be most likely to identify more readily a wolf or bear as a Dogman. They have a preconceived idea of what they already know and expect to see.

We know that fear-based responses can increase perception, and witnesses may see everyday events as unusual experiences. This may cause a distorted view of reality, since the fight-or-flight physiological response can amplify sensory input. This will make it more probable that witnesses will misperceive their environment. Second, shared concern and dread about the Dogman mythos can develop into a self-reinforcing feedback loop. One where expectations and fears are based on other people's stories and accounts brings about those people's expectations and fears.

One science division also deals with cryptozoology, or the reality of animals whose legendary existence has no evidence. Although mainstream science doesn't hold cryptids as something they believe in, there is enough anecdotal evidence regarding Dogman stories. There is enough to show that there has to be something behind these stories that needs to be investigated. Genetic analysis techniques, monitoring technology, and environmental mapping can assist us in the future to determine whether an elusive species might be responsible for the myth. For example, DNA sampling and genetic sequencing can help to identify known species that are lurking in the background. While deployments of surveillance sensors and cameras can help us gain useful insights into animal movement and habitat utilization.

On the other hand, folklore provides a rich backdrop for the Dogman's existence, with the legend of werewolves and shapeshifters existing across cultures for centuries. These stories of people transforming into wolves or other creatures are present in European, Native American, and African traditions. But they usually act as a symbol of man's primal fears. In most of these myths, the werewolf or monster are a warning against the dangers of the unknown. It tells us to beware of the world about us and the beasts that dwell there.

The Navaho and Hopi Native American mythos describes supernatural creatures quite similar to the Dogman known as Skinwalkers. This adds credibility to the theory that these stories are founded on long-standing cultural belief systems and not fantasy. Such ancient tales include vital information about the cultural and religious practices of the native people and the importance of respecting and continuing traditional practice and knowledge. By looking at the cultural context of Dogman sightings, researchers can gain a better understanding of the symbolic and metaphorical meaning of this phenomenon. And how it represents the hopes, fears, and anxieties of human societies.

THE IMPORTANCE OF CONTINUING THE INVESTIGATION

Even after decades of investigation, the Dogman is still an enigma wrapped in a veil of curiosity and intrigue. Skeptics continue to argue that the inability to provide concrete physical evidence in the form of bones, DNA samples, or inconclusive images or videos denies the existence of the creature. While others point out that absence of evidence is not evidence of absence. Our planet continues to amaze us with the discovery of new, undiscovered species in remote areas, and the size of our unexplored world is awe-inspiring. Just like the mouse lemur discovered by Dr. Mireya Mayor in 2000. This would be a perfect example of this. Before her expedition, this tiny primate had never been documented by science. This is how much we think we know and what yet remains unknown waiting to be discovered.

If Dogman is a living, breathing flesh and blood creature, then it could very well be hiding in places where science has not yet reached. Places such as far-off wildernesses, thick forests, or even parts of some suburban regions of large cities. Dogman's elusive and solitary nature is most likely the best reason for having no physical evidence. Better research tools are provided by new technology. It enables researchers to use new technologies and methods to find and examine potential evidence. Drone monitoring, camera traps, and artificial intelligence pattern detection can detect and follow up on possible sightings. Follow-up DNA analysis of hair, scat, blood, or environmental samples can yield genetic markers that suggest an undiscovered species.

Until this proof is discovered, the scientific community will not be quick to accept the Dogman as anything other than myth or misidentification. But the value of research goes beyond confirming or refuting the creature's existence. The Dogman phenomenon informs us about human psychology, cultural myth, and the nature of belief. By learning why individuals experience such things, what feelings are associated with them, and how rumors spread, scientists will be better able to understand how myths are created. And then, maybe why do certain legends endure throughout time.

Our storytelling ability and human imagination are the main reasons Dogman continues to live in contemporary popular culture. The creature's ability to draw upon our deepest fears and anxieties. And our interest in the supernatural and the unknown have captivated individuals of various cultures and throughout centuries. The metaphorical and symbolic meaning of Dogman can be achieved in association with themes of transformation, duality, and breaking boundaries between human and beast. Analyzing the cultural surroundings in which people report Dogman sightings helps us better achieve the symbolic and metaphorical meaning of the phenomenon. This helps us understand how this phenomenon embodies hopes, fears, and worries of human societies.

Our search for the Dogman brings us back to the contradictions and mysteries of human existence. By accepting the unknown and the inexplicable, we learn more about ourselves and our place in the universe. Maybe the Dogman can never be proven to exist, but its significance in shaping our collective imagination and common sense cannot be overemphasized.

WHAT KEEPS US SEARCHING?

Our need for the Dogman legend is an age-old concept of human nature. It is our need to pursue explanations for the unknown. As long as there have been humans on this earth, men and women have been trying to discover a reason for the unknown through the means of myth, religion, or science. This innate desire to know what lies ahead led us to seek knowledge of the unknown through various means. We continue to try to solve the questions that have perplexed us for centuries. The Dogman represents our shared fear, the fear of the wild, the unknown animal, the creature that defies the set boundaries of nature. This primitive fear is a reminder of our position in the universe, an acknowledgment of the boundaries of our perception and the extent of the unknown.

This fascination is much of why we still keep looking for explanations for why the Dogman exists. It is something that has engaged people from all societies and throughout time. As humans sacrifice their lives to the quest for extraterrestrial beings, ghostly apparitions, or hidden civilizations, the quest for these cryptids such as the Dogman is the product of the same natural curiosity. The more that can be gleaned by study, the more elusive the mystery. This stimulates even more investigation and forging more into the legend. It is this querying and questioning that has been the hallmark of human progress. Constantly pushing us forward to uncover what is beyond our understanding and to push the limits of our knowledge.

But another reason that Dogman has survived is because it has become a part of contemporary language. Popular media, in the form of books, TV shows, radio shows, and internet sites, have kept the enigma at center stage. With each new report or comment, new theories are presented, adding further muck to the muddling of the debate. Social media allows for real-time sharing of an experience. It allows for convening a global platform for believers and non-believers alike who continue to ask questions and engage in arguments over this phenomenon. The global platform has created a rich and multi-faceted debate, one which also reflects the multi-faceted complexion of the various aspects of the Dogman phenomenon. From the scientific postulates to the symbolic and cultural representations, Dogman has become a global phenomenon, crossing boundaries as much as cultures.

Besides, the Dogman also represents what is still to be discovered and that not all in our own world have been categorized and counted. With growing urbanization bringing more human population into the center of the wilderness, there remain vast expanses of wild countries unscathed by the probing eye of humanity. Encounters with cryptids like the Dogman make us wonder if we truly understand that which we believe we do. This wonder and awe are a part of our human nature. One that has propelled us to seek out and discover throughout the centuries. By accepting the mystery of the Dogman, we are encouraged to protect our natural world, honor the unknown, and to continue to discover.

FINAL THOUGHTS

Whether the Dogman is an unknown species, a psychic phenomenon, an interdimensional being, or a folkloric creature, its presence in the imagination and culture of human beings cannot be challenged. The myth survives because it resonates with something deep within us about human nature. In times of uncertainty, we are forced to question, to investigate, and try to understand things. This heightened curiosity has driven us to seek what cannot be explained. We still try to unravel the mysteries that have troubled us throughout history. Legends like Dogman bring us back to the intricacy and mystery of our existence and the reasons why we need to keep discovering and learning further.

Even if concrete evidence is scarce, the act of looking is extremely important. It keeps us actively involved in the mysteries of our existence. It expands the limits of our knowledge and imagination as well. The search for Dogman has inspired many to go into the unknown, go out into the woods, and find a new adventure. This feeling of discovery and adventure is one of the most fundamental things about human nature, and the Dogman myth has struck a chord within us.

Until the day that we will be able to say with certainty what the Dogman is or isn't a legend, we will keep on searching. We will urge future generations to search harder, listen more attentively, and never stop searching. It is a road of self-exploration, of discovery and of development. It is a reminder that there is always something new to find out, something new to know, and something new to learn about in our great and wonderful world.

The Dogman legend is a cultural reference, too, an image of man's imagination and the value in accepting what lies beyond. It has inspired thousands of works of art, literature, and musical pieces and is now a shared common heritage. The Dogman haunts us in our shared psyche, in whatever form we might envision him. A monster or creature of our fears and psyche. And so, the pursuit begins, prompted by our natural curiosity and desire to penetrate the secret of our own existence. Only time will tell what can be discovered.

BIBLIOGRAPHY

Herodotus. (2005). *The Histories:* by Herodotus (Author), Donald Lateiner (Introduction), G. C. Macaulay (Translator)

An essential source for understanding ancient accounts of exotic peoples and creatures, including early references to dog-headed beings such as the Cynocephali.

Pliny the Elder. (1969). *The Natural History* (J. Bostock & H. T. Riley, Trans.). Cambridge, MA: Harvard University Press.

This monumental work provides insights into ancient natural philosophy and early descriptions of unusual creatures, forming a backdrop for later mythological interpretations.

Redford, D. B. (Ed.). (2003). *The Oxford Essential Guide to Egyptian Mythology.* Oxford, UK: Oxford University Press.

A comprehensive reference on Egyptian deities such as Anubis, whose jackal-headed iconography offers parallels to later interpretations of canine humanoid figures.

Wilkinson, R. H. (2003). *The Complete Gods and Goddesses of Ancient Egypt.* New York: Thames & Hudson.

Provides detailed descriptions and cultural contexts for Egyptian deities that influence modern depictions of cryptid creatures.

Coleman, L., & Clark, J. (2002). *The Field Guide to Cryptozoology: A Natural History of Hidden Animals.* New York: Fireside.

A seminal work that offers a broad overview of cryptids worldwide, placing creatures like the Dogman within a wider context of unexplained phenomena.

Coleman, L. (1999). *Cryptozoology: Science, Myth, and the Pursuit of the Unknown.* New York: HarperCollins.

Explores the intersection of scientific inquiry and myth-making, and discusses both the methodology and challenges of studying creatures that have eluded conventional biology.

Smith, A. (2008). "From Myth to Science: The Evolution of Cryptozoology." *Cryptid Quarterly,* 2(3), 34–56.

An article that traces the evolution of cryptozoology as a field, examining how folklore transforms into scientific inquiry as new evidence and methods emerge.

Thompson, L. (2013). "Folklore and Cryptozoology: Understanding the Dogman Phenomenon." *Folklore Studies Journal,* 7(1), 89–105.

Focuses on the cultural and psychological dimensions of Dogman legends, offering a framework for understanding how local myths persist and evolve.

Zank, G. (2012). "Cryptids: The Intersection of Myth and Science." In *Mysterious Creatures of the Night.* New York: Random House.

A narrative-driven exploration of various cryptids that situates the Dogman within a broader tapestry of mysterious creatures.

VanLehn, S. (2004). "The Michigan Dogman: Legend or Reality?" *Journal of Midwest Cryptid Studies, 8*(4), 78–94.

An in-depth study examining the specific case of the Michigan Dogman, its origins, and its impact on local folklore and popular culture.

Fleischmann, M. R. (1991). *Beast of Bray Road: Tailing Wisconsin's Werewolf.* Milwaukee, WI: North Star Press.

Documents sightings and local lore surrounding the Beast of Bray Road, a legend that shares many similarities with the Dogman phenomenon.

Haggard, D. (2015). *Encounters with the Unknown: Eyewitness Accounts of the Dogman.* New World Press.

A compilation of firsthand accounts that investigates the consistency and variability in eyewitness testimonies regarding Dogman encounters.

Wilson, C. T. (2017). "DNA Testing in Cryptozoology: New Techniques and Challenges." *Journal of Molecular Mysteries, 5*(2), 112–130.

Explores modern DNA testing methods applied to cryptid research, discussing both the promise and the pitfalls of these techniques in verifying unknown samples.

Roberts, H. (2011). "The Science of the Unseen: Technological Advances in Cryptid Research." *Advances in Field Biology, 15*(3), 245–260.

Reviews how advances in imaging technology, field recording, and genetic analysis are transforming the way researchers study elusive creatures.

O'Connor, P. (2016). "Bipedal Beasts: A Comprehensive Look at Cryptid Adaptations." *Journal of Unexplained Phenomena, 9*(2), 201–220.

Investigates the anatomical and ecological plausibility of bipedal cryptids, offering comparative analyses with known animal species.

Levine, J., & Martin, S. (2019). "The Role of Cultural Memory in Cryptid Legends." *Journal of Mythological Studies, 14*(1), 55–75.

Discusses how collective memory and cultural narratives shape the formation and persistence of cryptid legends like the Dogman.

Dunbar, M. (2005). "An Analysis of Eyewitness Testimonies in Cryptid Encounters." *Psychology and the Paranormal, 3*(1), 76–95.

Analyze the psychological factors that influence eyewitness accounts, including memory bias, suggestibility, and the power of expectation.

McGinnis, M. (2018). "Investigating the Beast of Bray Road." *Journal of Cryptid Research, 12*(3), 150–169.

A study that looks at the interplay between local folklore, media coverage, and individual perception in shaping Dogman narratives.

Baker, J. (2020). "The Mystery of the Dogman: A Modern Myth." *Journal of Paranormal Research, 11*(4), 101–119.

Offers a synthesis of myth, science, and personal testimony to explore how modern society constructs and perpetuates the legend of the Dogman.

O'Connor, P. (2016). "Bipedal Beasts: A Comprehensive Look at Cryptid Adaptations." *Journal of Unexplained Phenomena, 9*(2), 201–220.

Addresses evolutionary biology questions by comparing cryptid features with those of known species, questioning whether unknown adaptations could exist in today's ecosystems.

Godfrey, Linda S. *The Beast of Bray Road: Tailing Wisconsin's Werewolf.* Stackpole Books, 2003.

A foundational investigation into Dogman and werewolf sightings in Wisconsin.

Godfrey, Linda S. *Real Wolfmen: True Encounters in Modern America.* Tarcher Perigee, 2012.

Expands on the Dogman phenomenon with first-person accounts and analysis.

MonsterQuest. Created by Doug Hajicek, History Channel, 2007–2010.

Television series that investigated cryptids, including the Gable Film and Dogman phenomenon.

The Bray Road Beast. Directed by Seth Breedlove, Small Town Monsters, 2018.

Documentary exploring the legendary creature in Elkhorn, Wisconsin.

The Dogman Triangle: Werewolves in the Lone Star State. Directed by Seth Breedlove, Small Town Monsters, 2023.

Documents sightings of Dogman-like creatures across Texas.

Dogman. Directed by Richard Brauer, Brauer Productions, 2012.

Dogman 2: The Wrath of the Litter. Directed by Richard Brauer, Brauer Productions, 2014.

Fictional horror films inspired by the Dogman legend.

The Beast of Bray Road. Directed by Leigh Scott, The Asylum, 2005.

A fictionalized horror take on the Bray Road phenomenon.

Cook, Steve. *The Legend.* WTCM-FM, 1987.

A radio song that sparked modern Dogman sightings and public fascination.

YouTube Channels:

Dark Waters

Mr. Ballen

Bedtime Stories

These content creators popularized cryptid narratives through dramatic storytelling and witness retelling.

North American Dogman Project (NADP). Founded by Joedy Cook.

A central group compiling and investigating Dogman sightings across North America.

Virginia Dogman Research (VDR).

Regional chapter of NADP involved in cryptid investigation within Virginia.

Reddit, TikTok, YouTube, and Facebook Cryptid Communities.

Platforms where modern Dogman stories, evidence, and legends are widely shared and debated.

Mayor, Mireya. "Mouse Lemur Discovery." 2000.

Referenced in the manuscript to support the plausibility of discovering new species.

ABOUT THE AUTHOR

Dr. W.J. (Bill) Brendle is a paranormal scholar and historian of the unseen who examines how belief in extraordinary phenomena shapes crime, culture, and identity. His work focuses on documented cases, folklore, and high-strangeness events that challenge conventional explanations while revealing deeper truths about human psychology and moral conflict. What began as an early fascination with unexplained experiences evolved into a disciplined pursuit of historical records, court transcripts, and cultural narratives that trace the real-world consequences of belief.

He holds a Ph.D. in Metaphysics with a specialization in parapsychology and has spent decades researching cryptid traditions, witchcraft history, esoteric systems, and unexplained phenomena. His work reflects both lived engagement with occult traditions and sustained historical study, allowing him to approach the unexplained with intellectual rigor and firsthand insight.

Brendle is the author of *Cryptids & Monsters of North Carolina* and *Heretics of the Harvest Moon: The True Story of the Witch Trials*. He is also the writer, producer, and co-host of the *4 Ever Paranormal* podcast, where stories of the strange are explored with atmosphere, scholarship, and an eye toward truth.

ALSO BY W.J. BRENDLE, PH.D.

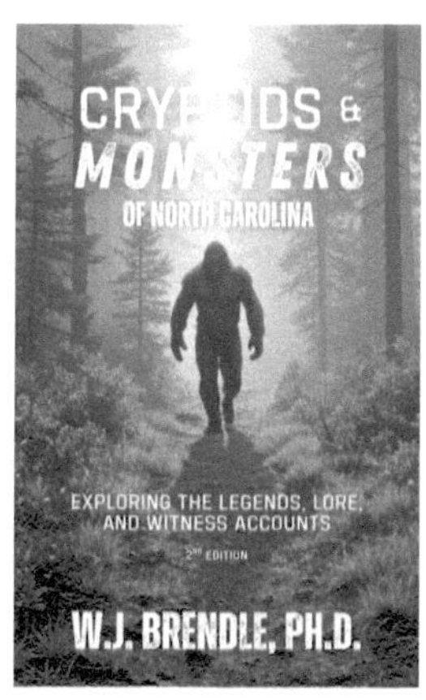

www.ingramcontent.com/pod-product-compliance
Lightning Source LLC
LaVergne TN
LVHW090520110826
845146LV00003B/925

* 9 7 9 8 8 9 2 3 4 1 5 1 6 *